T0130531

Got Carrots?
Rescued Horse

The Trail Ride

Patti Dammier

GOT CARROTS? RESCUED HORSE
THE TRAIL RIDE

iUniverse books may be ordered through booksellers or by contacting:

iUniverse
1663 Liberty Drive
Bloomington, IN 47403
www.iuniverse.com
1-800-Authors (1-800-288-4677)

ISBN: 978-1-5320-2411-5 (sc)
ISBN: 978-1-5320-2412-2 (e)

Library of Congress Control Number: 2017907717

Print information available on the last page.

iUniverse rev. date: 05/22/2017

Harley and Henry, part of the wonderful team; greatly missed

Contents

CHAPTER 1
Spring Everywhere

Spring for the Wild Horses

Spring was everywhere. The long, dreary, snowy days were fading, and the thawing weather had begun. No longer did the horses have to dig under the snow to graze. At the edge of a small wooded area where the wild horses often took shelter, the heavy branches of the trees loaded with snow and ice dripped a steady flow of water. This water would provide moisture for the new growing grass and provide lush fields for the herd. It had been a long winter, and the horses greeted the kinder weather with anticipation.

Many of the smaller animals that lived near the horses busied themselves with finding food that now was uncovered by the melting snow and digging neighbors. The woodland became similar to a busy day at the supermarket with hectic activity.

The herd sensed the change, and there seemed to be increased activity among the younger horses. This had been their first winter, and even though the first days were fun chasing snowflakes, the days grew colder and there was less grazing. Just like kids who initially thought only that snow meant playtime, the horses soon grew tired of searching for food by digging in the snow. When it seemed that winter would never end, the horses noticed a slight change in their surroundings. There was a renewed interest among the herd as the days grew longer and the sun again felt warm on their backs. The group stood contentedly in pairs, grooming each other by scratching the backs of their friends, The horses were less stressed in cold weather than in extreme heat. The youngsters had all fared well, and it seemed winter was nearing an end.

It had been a rare mild winter even though there was a lot of snow. This was preferable to past winters that had many subfreezing temperatures and several ice storms. The horses had eaten well during the past summer, when there was abundant lush grass. The extra layer of fat helped the horses by providing them with an extra layer of protection. They all had wonderful winter hair that became a little oily, helping to repel the snow off their backs. Longer sunny days, besides making all the horses feel friskier, helped them to start shedding their winter hair. Most outdoor horses have the ability to fluff out their hair with the ability of trapping warm air inside their coats. Often their domesticated blanketed relatives are less warm, especially if the blankets become dirty. The horses' hair often becomes matted, preventing their ability to fluff up their fur.

Life was peaceful and calm, and the days grew longer. The longer days would produce more grass and plentiful grazing for the horses. As the snow receded, more pasture became available. In the distance the small mountains could be seen outlined with the remaining white snow. Occasionally a loud noise was heard in the distance as the heavy ice and accumulated snow melted, breaking away and rolling down the side of the mountains. This caused a momentary alert as the horses looked to see what the leader was doing. When they saw that he relaxed and went back to grazing, they all relaxed too.

Each day brought less snow on the meadowland, although there was still some in the shaded areas. The tree glade still had some snow because of the shade and cooler temperature. The seemingly unending gray snowy days that had stretched into weeks now had a bright outlook with sunnier skies and longer days. Spring was a nice time of year for the herd. The younger horses suddenly felt energetic, and there was much running, leaping about, and playful sparring.

Pairs of horses were grooming each other, standing side-by-side and nuzzling each other's back. The mutual grooming helped in the shedding and discarding of their thick winter coats, especially on their backs. Occasionally, horses would use low hanging branches to scratch the hard-to-reach places of their backs. Life for the herd was getting easier with the diminished hardships of winter; without understanding why, the herd was more relaxed and comfortable. Meanwhile for Annie and Cassie, the weather didn't seem to be getting more springlike.

CHAPTER 2
Plans for Another Flight

Flight Plans

"Wow, it's going to pour," complained Cassie as they walked the dogs. She stopped and pulled her coat closed and buttoned up her hood in preparation for the rain. "This doesn't feel like spring." Annie Armstrong and Cassie Kelly had a pet care business, and part of their service was to exercise dogs for pet owners who worked and weren't able to take their animals out for walks.

Cassie continued her complaint about the weather. "I hope it won't be this cold for our spring vacation at Rolling Hills. I'm really looking forward to the trail ride they have planned." Again she wrapped her jacket tightly around her and buckled the belt. "It's sure cold for spring," she said, shivering.

Today they were taking care of two beautiful Great Danes named Harley and Henry. Even though both dogs were happy inside, they loved it when Annie and Cassie took them on long walks. Today's walk would have to be shorter because of the weather.

"Well, we still have over a month before the Rolling Hill's riding vacation, and by then we should be over these cold, unpredictable early spring showers." Annie picked up the pace for walking the dogs. The two Danes started a brisk trot with their long legs covering one stride for several quick steps by the girls. This brisk pace got them back home just before a cold, heavy downpour started. They quickly brought the dogs inside and began to prepare their meal. Harley was already standing in the kitchen with her bowl. She was very smart and would bring her bowl when it was time to eat.

"That was close. I sure hope this stops before we have to walk home," lamented Cassie as she peered out the kitchen window.

"We can wait a bit until it stops … doesn't look like it's more than a brief rainstorm" said Annie. "Anyway, we'll have a little time to talk about our plans."

Rolling Hills Equestrian Center Plans

The girls were planning their third session at the Rolling Hills Equestrian Center, where they had spent vacations learning about horses and various riding disciplines. Their first vacation had been spent learning about the art of driving horses and the use of special training carriages. The girls had become close friends after they were assigned as roommates their first summer vacation at Rolling Hills. After they found out that they lived fairly close to each other, they spent more time together learning about animals and earning extra money by caring for people's pets. The plan was to earn enough money to spend spring vacation continuing their horse adventures. They were both excited about the upcoming vacation because they would continue their riding lessons, but also there was an exciting trail ride with a camping trip planned to visit another farm near the school.

"Oh, look—it's stopping." The girls hurried and tidied up the kitchen where they had prepared the dogs' meal, and gave each dog a biscuit and a pat. The dogs settled down to chew on their favorite bones. "We can probably make it to my house before it starts to rain again," said Annie as the girls quickly tossed on raincoats and headed home. Cassie was going to spend the night so they could work on several plans. The continuing rainstorm was so strong it made a loud noise as it hit the roof.

"Hi Mom," called Annie as the girls rushed through the door, escaping getting soaked as another downpour started.

"You girls made it just in time," Annie's mother greeted them. "You didn't get too wet while walking the dogs, did you? That rain sounds horrible."

"We had barely enough time to get them home before that last downpour, but we made it," said Cassie, who sounded as though she had run all the way.

"Well, I guess you worked up a good appetite. Dad is running late with his flight because of this weather ... the flight was delayed, so we'll start without him." Annie's dad was a pilot with an airline, but flew smaller planes as well. It was a great adventure, flying with Annie's parents. Annie's mother also had a pilot's license to fly small planes. Her parents had met while she was taking flying lessons. Annie was also learning to fly and even Cassie had a chance to fly on their last trip to see the wild horses. Cassie was new to flying, but since her first flight, when they had flown to see where the wild horses roamed, she could hardly wait to fly again.

Annie and Cassie busied themselves helping to get dinner ready. The conversation was all about the vacation plans at Rolling Hills. Annie's mom hinted that there were also some plans to do another flying trip.

Annie and Cassie looked at each other with happy surprise. "Where are we going? When are we going?" they asked.

Annie's mom smiled and said, "Wait and see ... it's a surprise."

There was much interesting conversation with lots of questions about the surprise, but Annie's mom was secretive and would say only that they had to wait and find out. When they finished dinner, the girls helped put things away and straightened up the kitchen. Part of the dinner was put aside for Annie's dad. They went upstairs to Annie's room to work on their school science project and discuss the upcoming surprise trip. This next trip was probably going to be to another place that had something to do with horses. Now the girls turned their attention to all the material they had gathered on their last trip for their end-of-school science presentation about the development of the horse.

Suddenly Cassie changed the subject and remarked, "What do you think the wild horses are doing?"

Last year the family had flown a small plane to an archaeological equine site that contained one of the largest collection of horse fossils. They had gathered a lot of information for their science project. The trip had been the first time that Cassie had flown in a small airplane, which had opened a new exciting adventure. Since Annie's dad was an airline pilot and her mother also had a pilot's license, flying came easy to the family, including Annie. Even though she wasn't old enough to have a pilot's license, she could fly a flight plan under her dad's supervision. Annie was already an accomplished pilot and looking forward to completing the requirements for a license when she turned seventeen years old. On the return trip they had flown over the area where wild horses roamed.

The Wild Horses

They turned their attention to thinking about the wild horses. "Remember there was a lot of snow when we went for the sleigh rides down at the edge of the farm where the wild horses often came for hay that was placed in the hayracks?" Thoughtfully Annie said, "I know they at least had some extra food to count on."

Cassie continued, "It's lucky our 'mystery mare' was found before the winter snowstorms started."

The girls had flown over the edge of the farm where the wild horses lived and landed on a nearby farm's dirt landing strip so they could get a closer look. They had also wanted to show the horses to Annie's parents. What they found was a big surprise. One of the horses was injured and stood alone, unable to keep up with the herd. It was lucky they had discovered her and alerted the farm owner about the injured horse. The farm workers looked after the wild horses that often came near the lower pastures. They would put out food when the weather made it difficult for them to find food on their own. The farm team brought the transport trailer down from the farm, where the injured mare stood.

What happened next was a surprise to all. The mare was apprehensive but allowed the rescue team to approach her. What happened next was even more surprising: the mare confidently walked right into the trailer with no apparent fear. As the mare was taken care of and her injuries healed, a remarkable discovery was made about her and one of the young wild horses that had been found after it was abandoned in a dreadful storm the previous year. The tiny filly had been found when the campers had planned a picnic several days after the storm. She was nearly dead from the ordeal, but with round-the-clock care, in which Annie and Cassie assisted, returned the little horse to excellent health.

Some interesting things happened between the lost filly and the hurt mare. The filly had been found on the picnic outing at the lower edge of the farm. That was the beginning of uncovering the true story of what everyone began to call the Mystery Mare.

CHAPTER 3
Flying to Horse Island

Flight Plans

Their discussion about the wild horses was interrupted by a call from Annie's mother downstairs. "Take a break and come downstairs for a bit. Your dad just arrived home, and he wants to tell you about our flying plans." The girls quickly gathered up their belongings, piled them neatly in the storage container, and hurried downstairs to hear the news.

Cassie was excited about the future trip. This was a change from her previous apprehension on their first flight. On that trip, she had sat in the front seat of the airplane with Annie's dad. Not only did she have a great view, but she also had a chance to take the controls and fly the plane. She now was enthusiastic about flying and couldn't wait for the next chance to fly.

Annie's dad had a flight map laid out on the table when the girls walked into the dining room. Her parents were discussing things on the map. They looked up when the girls entered and pointed at the large map. "What do you think about a trip to this island?" The girls seated themselves at the large table and followed the straight lines of the plastic ruled plotter that her dad had placed on the map.

Both girls were already starting to practice plotting a course for a flight and recognized the plastic piece that Annie's dad was using, called a plotter. It allowed pilots to plan the mileage and make accurate calculations about a cross-country trip. Important information about the directions and compass headings helped the pilots know which direction to fly the plane. All this preparation was important and took careful planning, which the girls took seriously.

"This is our final destination," Annie's father said, pointing at the map, "and this is where we're starting. So ... how do we plan our trip?" He smiled knowingly at his wife, waiting to see what the girls would say.

Annie and Cassie moved closer to the table and started discussing how they would plan the trip to the island and find the airport. While they worked on the problem, Annie's mom started to give them hints about the "special island." "I know you girls are going to love visiting this island, because it is unique and one of the only places in the whole world that has no cars. Once we land at the airport, we will not see any motor-driven vehicles."

"What!"

"How is that, like ... possible?"

"You'll find out," she said with a teasing laugh. "Now, here are some things I would like you to do to find out about this special island. This island has a lot of history, and it's very interesting how it came about that there are only horses for transportation." The girls looked at each other with disbelief. They both started to ask questions at once.

"Dad," Annie said, "how did it happen that this island doesn't have any cars and has stayed using only horses?" She paused to think and then said, "Absolutely no vehicles are allowed?"

"Well, all the people on the island decided that they wanted to keep it the same, so laws were passed that prohibited any vehicles on the island," her dad replied. "Once we land at the airport, we will have to travel by horse."

"Wow, this sounds so wonderful," Cassie said, sighing. "A place where there are only horses."

"They allow bicycles, and there are several large fire trucks and emergency vehicles, but those are the only exceptions," Annie's dad said. "It was decided that if there were a fire, it wouldn't be wise to limit the rescue with horses. Half of the island is a national park, and a small part north of the airport has a few private homes. It is a wonderful place to explore." He looked at the girls' excited faces and smiled at his wife, Mary. "We have a pilot friend who lives on the island during spring and summer. He and his wife run one of the small guesthouses. He also has one of the stables where several of his horses are kept. They provide outings for tourists to take rides in carriages around the island." He paused to let this last statement be heard and continued, "Seems like this might be an opportunity for some girls we know to practice their carriage-driving skills," he smiled, nodding to his wife.

Annie and Cassie heard the word *'horses'* and looked at each other in surprise, because this sounded almost as if it were a fairytale. An island where there were only horses. This was a dream come true.

"Mom and I thought that since the two of you enjoy horses so much, that this would be the perfect place for us to take a trip. We know how hard you both work to keep your grades up at school and also do your part-time work taking care of people's pets, and we want to encourage your love of animals. This trip will be a fun time for all of us and a chance for you to see some very large horses with carriages."

The Spring Storm

The days of spring were stretching into longer days of sunshine, and the herd of wild horses luxuriated in warm days of grazing. Today was like any other day's routine of grazing and walking to the lake to drink. The air hung heavy with large puffy clouds filling the sky. The peaceful-looking clouds clung to the small row of mountains that ran along a nearby ridge. Nothing seemed out of the ordinary, and the herd kept their normal movement and grazing pattern. Unfortunately, the area was vulnerable to changeable spring weather with alternating rain and windy wet snowstorms. There were also hail and thunderstorms, because the temperatures were so changeable. The temperature could change suddenly from warm sunshine to cold, wintery weather.

The air that had been warm suddenly turned cool as a series of large clouds moved in and covered the sunlight. As the bright sunshine disappeared, the horses lifted their heads, seeing the changing sky. Noticing the change, the horses intuitively began to move toward the shelter of the trees, turning their backs to the increasingly strong wind. The surrounding niche of trees gave some protection to the horses from the wind and sudden falling snow. This area was noted for quick changes in the weather, and sudden spring storms often caught the wild horses without shelter. This time the herd was lucky to be near a beautiful shelter of trees that protected them from both the wind and blowing snow. Many spring storms were short lived, and the horses were spared a long, uncomfortable night of huddling together for warmth and protection.

This sheltered area had another advantage. Besides the shelter of the trees, this area was close to the edge of the Rolling Hills Equestrian Center, which often supplied the wild horses with extra food piled in hayracks at the edge of the farm. With the additional help from the staff and students, the wild horses had an easier time when nature wasn't so kind. It sure didn't feel like spring.

While the wild horses doubted that spring was around the corner because of the sudden strange winter storms, both Annie and Cassie worried that their plans for a flight to the island of horses would be cancelled. But as luck would have it, there was a change in the weather, and the girls began their flight plans in earnest. They spent several sessions sitting at the table with Annie's parents, figuring out all the details of the flight plan. They plotted out the distance, and compass directions, including future weather forecasts for the time of their proposed flight. They both knew that at the last moment their plans could change, because as the wild horses experienced, spring weather is often unpredictable.

Weekend Flight to Horse Island

The weekend was rapidly approaching, and the weather forecast looked as if they would be able to make the trip happen. Annie and Cassie busied themselves with not only flight planning but also packing. Cassie's aunt Emma, with whom she had lived since the death of her parents, was also helping with the trip preparations. She had been a great help in introducing Cassie to a number of different interests by encouraging her with many wonderful activities. She had visited the Rolling Hills Equestrian Center a year earlier and enjoyed hearing about all the animals' adventures, especially the happenings with the wild horses. She was pleased that Cassie had made some wonderful friends and was excited about her new adventures. It was good for Cassie to be involved with new people.

The flight plans continued as Annie and Cassie worked hard to make the necessary preparations and keep up with schoolwork and their pet care service. They were indeed busy. While they sat together one evening, Annie's dad said, "You know, even though we will be flying over a short stretch of water to land on the island, we'll have to have other safety gear on board, so this means that our total weight will have to include this extra gear." He looked knowingly at the girls and said in a mockingly stern voice, "Absolutely no twenty-pound bags of carrots!" The girls burst out laughing at his joke and thought of their care of the rescued filly, whose name was Got Carrots. She had learned all her manners by getting a carrot treat for learning new behavior.

The girls had learned much from working with the young horse in addition to their regular lessons and equestrian studies. They had taught her to wear her halter and pick up her feet for cleaning. She loved being brushed. It would almost be one year since she was discovered at the edge of the farm, nearly dead from exposure and lack of food. She was too young to survive on her own without her mother. With good care she was now growing strong and healthy.

Horses need to be handled in a consistent manner with orderly training. Miss Katy, who was a school instructor had helped Annie and Cassie begin working with the rescued filly, Got Carrots, but now there would be more lessons for both the girls and the little filly.

CHAPTER 4

The Flight to Horse Island

Flight Day

Finally the day came for the flight to Horse Island. The weather was perfect, and all the plans were in place for the cross-country flight. A cross-country flight includes a flight from one airport and includes a landing at another, and the calculations for the route. The girls had prepared the route and made the needed calculations using what they had learned about wind direction and their planned course to the island.

Small planes are sensitive to wind, so the weather had to be seriously considered. They also considered each person's weight and the weight of all their items. Since they would be flying over water to the island, they had to include extra emergency equipment.

"How's all the planning going?" Annie's dad asked.

"I think we're ready to have you check what we've done," Annie said.

Her dad sat down at the table and pulled out his plotter so he could check the lines the girls had drawn showing the plane's route to the Horse Island Airport. "You're getting real good at this," he said, nodding to the girls. "Okay, now how about the weight … remember we have to take the extra emergency equipment. It's good the two of you are as light as you are," he said with a laugh. "We can pack more stuff. Have you checked the weather?"

"It looks as if we're in luck. We have a good forecast," said Annie.

"Now off to get a good night's sleep … tomorrow will be a long day."

The girls gathered and organized all their things and stored them neatly for the next day's flight. Cassie was staying over so they could get an early start. Normally they would talk about all their animals and neat things they were doing, including their pet care service. But tonight they were sound asleep in minutes.

Perfect Weather

The day was sunny with clear skies. It was a perfect day for their trip. Everyone scurried around gathering what was needed for the trip. After a hearty breakfast, they were off to the airport. After sorting everything out and getting things stored for the flight once more, Cassie thought, *… Here I am … going to fly.*

"Okay, Cassie, it's your turn in the front seat," she heard Annie's dad say.

Oh wow, I'm so nervous, she thought.

"Now Cassie don't worry about a thing, … remember how much fun it was."

Everyone was in a seat with the seat belt on when Annie's dad yelled, "Clear." This call was made to ensure that no one was near the plane before the engine was started. The group had performed the checks on all the critical items needed to fly.

In what seemed like a matter of seconds they were rushing down the runway and in the air, looking down at the cars, houses, and people becoming smaller and smaller. Cassie had a great view out the front window when she heard the directions, "What is your heading?"

She immediately looked down at her flight plan and said, "Heading thirty-five degrees."

She had studied all the plans that would allow the pilot to know which direction to fly the plane. Part of being a student pilot was learning to navigate the flight plan using a map and a planned route telling the pilots the direction to fly. The girls had seriously planned the whole trip to Horse Island, and the first direction was to fly the compass heading of the numbers for the direction of thirty-five degrees on the instrument that they were reading.

"Good," Annie's dad said. "I'll get the plane's controls set to fly in the directions you and Annie planned, and then you can take the control yoke."

The plane had what looked to be two half steering wheels in the front seats where Cassie and Annie's dad were flying the plane. Cassie was getting ready to take hold of one of the controls so she could fly the direction that they had planned.

"Ready?" Annie's dad asked.

Cassie looked serious, and concentrated on the circle of numbers on the instrument panel in front of her. The numbers moved around in a circle as the plane changed its course, so she had to concentrate so she could keep the plane headed in the direction toward the island. She put her hands on the controls and started to steer the course. The controls had a variety of movements that turned left and right to turn the plane, but this control also could be pulled or pushed to make the plane go up or down. The coordination of those different directions took student pilots many hours of supervised training with an instructor pilot. Cassie made the correct movements to turn the plane to the correct numbers on the compass heading, but she put just a little too much pressure on the control that that caused the plane to start pointing slightly down.

She looked concerned, but Annie's dad immediately helped her feel the right pressure by taking his yoke and pulling back slightly. She could feel the corrections on her yoke control because both the steering controls were connected.

"See how easy that is?"

Cassie suddenly relaxed and smiled, "Yes, that's great that you can show me the corrections with your control … wow … good to know I can't make a big mistake."

Annie and her mom were in the backseats and offered their encouragement. Since Annie's mom was a pilot and Annie was also taking lessons, they knew how much concentration flying took. Time passed as they flew along this direction. Cassie suddenly called, "I see our next checkpoint … there is the beginning of the water where we'll turn for our next heading toward the island."

"Okay crew, let's check our time so we'll will know our speed and our next checkpoint," Annie's dad said.

Everyone checked the flight plan, and Annie said, "I think we have eight minutes until the next checkpoint."

Small planes unlike larger commercial planes don't have sophisticated navigational equipment, so pilots learn to fly by looking at points on the ground and checking them against the other calculations they've made in preparation for the flight. This navigation is call VFR, or visual flight reference, and an important part of learning to fly.

"All right, crew," Annie's dad said. "We all have to give our attention to the next checkpoints, because we're going to be leaving our last land visual checkpoint as we start over the water to the airport on Horse Island. It's only a short distance and will take only about ten minutes. We'll be able to see the land during the flight." He talked over their special headsets so the girls could learn some of the important parts about flying over water. "We've got clear weather, so we should see our island airport pretty soon. It should be to the right side of our plane, because it's toward the upper left side of the island. Everyone keep your eyes sharp."

After about ten minutes they could see the outline of the tiny island airport. "Our checkpoint has worked perfectly," Annie's dad said, "so Cassie is going to change her heading to the direction of fifty-six degrees … this means we will turn slightly to the right, approaching with the island on the right side of the plane, and set up our approach to land at the airport." Everyone listened carefully as he explained the next part of the trip.

View of Horse Island

The island was now in full view, and they could see the many buildings that lined the shore. They could also see one of the big hotels on the point of the island that they would use for a visual checkpoint. The girls were excited as they flew closer and could see more details. They could see that part of the island had many buildings, but the other part was densely covered with trees and appeared unpopulated, with no sign of buildings. As Annie's dad started to fly the approach to the airport, they could see more of what was happening on the ground.

"Look at all those horses and carriages going down the street," exclaimed Cassie.

"There isn't a car to be seen anywhere," said Annie to her mom. "It's just like you described."

They were now low enough to see the island and details below. Their path changed, and they started flying away from the populated area toward what was described as a national park. That was where many of the visitors took horse-and-carriage tours or people who owned horses rode them. The island wasn't more than several miles traveling all the way around on the few existing roads.

Annie's dad announced that they were getting ready to land as he turned the plane to line up on the small airport that was visible in the clearing ahead. Normally Annie's mom would talk on the radio to the tower and get permission to land. This airport, however, had no tower since there were hardly any planes landing, so the pilots were responsible for announcing over the radio that they intended to land.

Everyone looked around to see if any planes were flying in the island area. Not a plane was in sight. Annie's dad announced on the radio the number on the plane and the direction from which they were landing. Minutes later, they glided slowly downward, and then the plane gently touched down on the runway.

There at the end of the runway they could see two large horses with a beautiful carriage. The girls spotted the horses right away as Annie's dad slowly and carefully taxied the plane to the parking area off to the side before coming to a final stop. "Oh, do you see that?" commented Cassie. Sitting in the carriage, a figure waved.

Cassie looked out the window. "The horses look like that large horse we helped guide for the costumed rider in the parade. Remember how big he was and how he kept trying to eat the flowers on the queen's carriage? Big Gray was very well-behaved even when his bridle broke," she remembered. The girls had assisted walking horses during a parade to help the young riders in the saddle keep a slow parade pace.

Chapter 5

Visit to Horse Island

Fun Horse Adventure

Annie's dad turned their attention back to the task at hand, "Let's get the plane parked and tied down and we'll introduce you to our friend, Bob Wright ... oh yes ... and the horses," he added with a laugh. The job was done quickly, and the group walked over to the waiting horses and carriage. Introductions were made all around, including the two large horses that stood waiting perfectly quietly while everyone's things were loaded into the big carriage. The girls walked in front of the horses and quietly took in the atmosphere of the beginning of another fun horse adventure.

"So, Bob, tell us about this new business that you and your lovely wife are doing have started here on Horse Island."

"Everybody climb in and I'll tell you how this all started," Bob said. Turning to the girls, he asked, "How would you like to sit up here next to me?"

They didn't need any more coaxing, and climbed into the carriage, sitting on either side of Bob and right behind the two horses. He picked up what seemed like a bulky bunch of reins and turned to the group, "Everyone ready?"

The enormous horses heard Bob's command, "Walk on" and they effortlessly started the carriage moving. The girls noticed how large these horses were compared with those on the farm. They were taller and much more massive. It was going to be interesting to find out about these unique horses. Annie heard her dad talking to Bob and switched her focus from the horses walking in front of the carriage to the conversation.

"Well, Bob, this is certainly a wonderful venture with running a bed-and-breakfast," Annie's dad said. "Seems like a big change from flying planes."

"My wife and I decided that we needed a change of pace," Bob said. "As you and Mary know, this flying job is demanding, and we've always loved horses and living near the water. When a friend told me about this property, we decided to take a look at it. Horse Island operates for tourists ate spring until early fall. The hotels shut down and have a few folks to do maintenance. At that time all the horses go back to the mainland, because the weather becomes too difficult for year-round operation.

"Most of the tourists come by the ferry and occasionally by private boat. It's only a short distance between the mainland and the island. There are a few planes that come into this airport, but you can see by the size of the runway that they have to be fairly small— private planes like you folks." He paused and encouraged the horses to pick up the pace. "These two big boys will go back with us with all the other horses that are on the island. October is when the island officially closes for tourism and basically becomes a ghost town. It can be extremely difficult to live here during the winter, but this time of year it is wonderful."

The words *ghost town* got both the girls' attention. They remembered all their adventures touring in the national park that had the biggest collection of horse fossils in the world. In the surrounding area were many ghost towns that had once been mining towns. They had studied the history of the remains of those now unpopulated settlements.

"How do the horses get back to the mainland?" Cassie questioned, changing the subject back to horses.

"There are large commercial ferries that take the horses back, because there are hundreds of horses here on the island. As you folks will see, the horses are the only means of transportation, except for the few emergency vehicles."

There was a moment of silence as the girls thought about the island operating with only horses for transportation. This was unbelievable, and one of the few places in the whole world where horses still reigned supreme. What a wonderful place to spend a short vacation—with horses and the sounds of hoof beats.

Annie asked, "Does that mean that all the work on the island is done using horses and carriages?"

"Yes," Bob replied. "It means that once supplies for the hotels arrive by ship, they're delivered by horses. Not only are people transported, but their entire luggage is too. It's quite something to see. There are some bicycles but no motor-driven vehicles."

The horses quietly moved the carriage through the wooded area near the airport and came to a road in an open area. The small island had several different types of landscapes. On one side of the island a trail ran near the rocky beach with a beautiful view of the water. As the trail turned away from the water toward the center of the island, the scene changed from the coastline to a forest with many trees. Folks driving carriages had to pay close attention to the map they carried so they wouldn't become confused by the various changes in the trails. At this midpoint, some of the trails went to the farthest point of the island, which was a national parklands, or continued around to the center and back to the main town where all the hotels and stores were.

Center of the Island

The small airport was at the center of the island where the dense trees opened up onto bright grassy fields. The group was heading to a location between the town and the small airfield. The part of the island closest to the mainland was lined with beautiful shore-view hotels. Some were extremely old and had a historic significance from the time of the beginning of the United States. There was an old fort, and there were beautiful scenic places that looked out to the sea.

A road, starting in the town where the ferries arrived, went all the way around the edge of the island and had a wonderful view of the water on one side with the meadows and woodlands on the other. The spacious, comfortable, distinctive cottage that Bob and his wife had bought was at the edge of the national park, so they were away from the main streets where the horses and carriages paraded back and forth, taking the hotels' guests on scenic rides around the island. It was the perfect place for a relaxing, peaceful vacation. They hoped the small inn would develop into the perfect resort for folks who wanted to get away from the city and spend some quiet time. The major hotels at the edge of the island, overlooking the water, had lots of activity with more tourists.

Suddenly the girls heard Bob say, "So, when are you two pilots ready for a tour around the island? I heard that the two of you, besides studying flying, are working hard to become accomplished riders."

They both started talking at the same time, but Cassie started laughing and said, "You go first."

"Okay, I'll start and then you finish," Annie said, nodding in Cassie's direction. "We just finished several riding sessions at an equestrian school, where we learned about many of the horse disciplines. It's also a full-time school for older students who want to become licensed in the equestrian disciplines while they're finishing their high school diplomas. One of the last classes we took was on working with a small horse and carriage."

She turned and looked at Cassie as if to say *You take over.* Cassie took the lead. "It was a lot of hard work to learn all the parts of the small carriages and harnesses. We also took a second class where they changed the small carts that had wheels into sleighs."

"Way cool," said Bob. "How did they do that?"

"Well, it was really a mystery at first," Cassie said as they all listened, even though everyone except Bob knew the story. "The little carriages were small carts that had two wheels."

Cassie and Annie both explained that they were really large bicycle wheels. "To make the carts into sleighs, we attached these pieces of metal that looked like candy canes over the wheels so they became sleighs," Cassie said. She stopped and looked at the faces smiling approval at her description of the cart transformation.

"Well, I'll be darned," Bob said. "If that doesn't beat all. I never heard about carriages being turned into sleighs. That's one of the best horse-and-carriage stories I've heard." He turned and looked at the girls and said, "You two are going to have a fun time here. You'll have to meet Rocky, one of the big horses that pulls a single carriage."

As the group came around the drive with the small farm in front of them, Annie and Cassie grinned at each other: they knew they were going to have another wonderful horse adventure.

CHAPTER 6
Meeting Rocky

Tour of Horse Island

Everyone was settled into their rooms and Annie's parents were off walking around the lovely gardens with Bob's wife, viewing the newly planted flowers and trees. The girls were admiring the horses in their stalls, and Bob was telling them about each of the large horses when he asked, "Who would like to take a short tour with a small carriage led by Rocky?" He pointed to a beautiful large horse known as a Clydesdale.

Clydesdales had become famous for pulling enormous loads in teams of several horses. They certainly were suited for taking the larger wagons around the village.

Cassie turned to Annie and said with awe, "He looks just like Big Gray, only he's a different color." Big Gray was the large horse that Annie had led with a rider in a parade. Bob led Rocky out of his stall where he was happily munching and brought him to a small carriage. Much of the harnessing was familiar with a few exceptions that Bob helped complete. After a short time with Bob giving Annie and Cassie directions, Rocky was harnessed and ready for the outing. Rocky waited patiently in front of the smartest, single-horse carriage as the three stepped into it. Bob sat between the two girls so they could see and take a turn driving. "You two have really learned your harnessing … Way cool."

"Ready," he called, and they were off for a short tour of the island. "I'm going to show you the major directions and where the main roads cross so you can get an idea of which road leads to different parts of the island. You remember you landed in a clearing that is approximately at the center of the island and divides the national park from the other section that is developed into hotels and homes." Annie and Cassie listened attentively, trying to remember how the island had looked as they landed. "We're going to head to the business part of the island and take a short ride around the town." He gave the command for Rocky to walk on, and the carriage easily started to move.

The scenery became more open with more buildings, and Bob described the historic buildings that were coming into view. "We're going to be driving past one of the oldest buildings on the island. It's a military fort. Look out that way and you'll see we have a clear view of the ocean overlooking the small town. You can see how the position of this fort would have helped protect the village from possible attack from approaching ships."

The view was spectacular as Rocky slowly brought the carriage onto one of the main streets. Buildings were everywhere and close together. The carriage began to approach a hill that had a magnificent hotel to the right and a park on the left. The road that had been empty of other carriages suddenly was a busy thoroughfare with large carriages filled with tourists. Rocky with the small carriage, moved into the long line of carriages that filled the street.

The girls didn't know which way to look next. "This big hotel on our right is famous. They even made a movie here." Bob directed their attention to the long curving drive that passed beautiful landscaped gardens and a grand veranda with another spectacular view. The garden had hedges that were shaped into horses. The long driveway that ran directly in front was lined with beautiful carriages to take the visitors around on tours. Their carriage continued down to the main part of town where the major ferries deposited visitors. The street was now really congested, and shops, small hotels, and restaurants were crowded next to each other.

The girls looked around nervously because it seemed that Rocky was very close to the other carriages. Bob noticed and quickly calmed their fears. "Rocky knows his way around this town—I'm sure he has the route memorized," he said with a laugh. "Rocky is way cool."

"The school horses at the farm where we learned to drive were knowledgeable too," said Cassie as she remembered how her driving horse partner would stop when she gave him a command he couldn't do. "If I tried to turn the carriage too sharply he seemed to know he couldn't make the turn. He would stop until our instructor came and straightened the carriage. It was a lot of fun, and I learned to make the turn more smoothly."

"It sounds as if you've had good instruction," Bob commented as he guided Rocky to turn into a road that led away from the town. "This road loops around the island and returns to where we started from. We could continue on this road that goes around through the national park. This is different from the part of the island we looked at. The road passes through dense trees and there are no buildings." Bob continued with a narrative about all the places they passed, and the girls tried to remember what he described.

Annie and Cassie Drive the Carriage

The carriage had left the town, and there were fewer carriages until the populated area disappeared and their carriage was the only one on the road. Bob turned to them and said, "Who's ready to drive Rocky?" Annie and Cassie looked shyly at each other, neither wanting to be first. "Okay," said Bob, "Annie can be first this time and Cassie the next time we drive." He handed the reins to Annie, who held them as she had been taught. Rocky didn't change his pace but kept walking steadily along.

They approached a fork in the road, and Bob explained that they should turn left to take them back to the house. If they continued more to the right, they would end up circling around the Park Forest. Annie carefully turned Rocky to the left, and he made the turn to head home. They came to a straight stretch in the road, and Bob turned to Cassie to let her take over. Cassie nervously took the reins and whistled a few bars of a little song. Cassie always quietly hummed when she felt uncertainly. Rocky kept walking along as if nothing had changed, and Cassie felt confident and relaxed. Bob noticed that she was enjoying driving Rocky. "See how easy this is? Just like back at your riding school with smaller horses."

"Wow, this is great," exclaimed Cassie, Way cool!" Bob and Annie laughed. The following days went by too quickly, and soon it was time to fly home. Annie's dad had a commercial flight, and the girls had school. They'd had lots of fun driving Rocky around the small island and seeing the beautiful views. It seemed as if they had only just arrived and already the foursome was back in the plane, getting ready for the return trip.

Annie and Cassie looked wistfully out the window at Bob and their new carriage horse friend, Rocky. Annie's mother sensed the girls' sadness and said cheerfully, "This is such a short flight … we can easily come back to visit Rocky. You both have to get ready for your next horse adventure, walking your dogs, the science fair …" Her voice trailed off with the long list of fun things.

CHAPTER 7

Return to Rolling Hills Equestrian Center

Return to Rolling Hills

The staff at Rolling Hills Equestrian Farm always planned exciting lessons and horse trips during the riders' stay. Throughout the year there was a full-time school program where the regular live-in students took the same classes they would take at any high school. The difference was that not only did they take their regular required classes, but they also learned about equine studies so that they could become licensed to run an equestrian center such as Rolling Hills.

During vacation times, many of the regular students went home, but many of the older ones stayed and instructed newly arrived campers as part of their graduation requirements. Younger students came during their regular vacations and studied various riding disciplines such as vaulting, driving carriages, and riding. They also participated in the school's other activities, learning stable management and horse care. Each of the younger students worked under the guidance of older students as they not only learned riding skills, but assisted in the feeding and care of the horses.

This spring was no different than from the other vacations scheduled during summer, fall, and winter. The students would take specialized classes and there would also be particular horse outings. During the previous winter's vacation not only did they take riding and horse-carriage driving lessons, but also they had a chance to turn their driving carts into small sleighs. This spring's vacation session would include many fun activities. After much planning, the day for the return trip to Rolling Hills finally came.

When the car came around the familiar bend, Cassie, Annie, Cassie's aunt Emma, and Annie's parents recognized the fields surrounding Rolling Hills. "Well, here we are again at Rolling Hills," said Annie's dad. Each time they came, the view was a little different. This time there was none of the heavy snow that had fallen during the winter vacation. Off in the distant hills they could see the remains of the light spring snowstorms that occasionally appeared as the warmer weather arrived.

"Do you know where you'll be staying?" asked Annie's mother.

"We've been assigned the same cabin as the summer and winter session—the one that looks out over the pasture," Cassie said.

"I can hardly wait to see all of our friends," Annie said. "I wonder how Jasmine the cat and all the horses are doing."

"I bet your little rescued horse is getting bigger," said her dad.

They drove up the tree-lined entrance and parked in front so the girls could go to the main hall and check-in. They let Annie and Cassie go off to get settled. This was always a noisy time as friends greeted each other and caught up on the latest news. "You know your way around," Annie called to her parents as they the girls excitedly hurried to meet their friends. "We'll meet you here in forty-five minutes for the group supper." Her parents had visited the farm and enjoyed the wonderful events and demonstrations, especially when the girls presented the little filly Got Carrots.

"Cassie, it looks like we're going to be with the same group," Annie said as they walked over to their assigned table and saw familiar faces.

Alex was one familiar smiling face. "Looks like we're going to be stuck with you two again," he laughingly said. "You must be doing the riding and trail course. I'm really looking forward to the overnight trail ride. That is going to be great."

All four of the students Cassie, Annie, Mike and Alex had been in two other sessions and had worked hard to learn the necessary basic riding skills to be competent on horseback. The foursome was going to be assigned the same group. During this riding session, they were going to get the opportunity to go on an overnight trail ride at the end of the spring classes. They sat at their usual meeting table and discussed all the happenings since their winter vacation course.

"Wait till we tell you about this great trip we took," said Cassie. "I got to fly again—it was way cool. We went with Annie's parents, who are pilots, and ..." She was about to finish when one of their favorite instructors appeared. The group had been fortunate to have Mr. Randall for all their classes. He was a wonderful storyteller and made all the classes fun, telling stories about his adventures in addition to all the information about horses. He had a turned-up mustache that made him look as if he was always smiling.

"Well, look who's here ... my favorite group of students." He looked around and noticed that they were missing one. "Where's Sherlock Holmes?" He was referring to Mike, who had helped solve the case of the missing cat, Jasmine. The girls had rescued Jasmine on their first trip to Rolling Hills, and she had become a noticeable member of the farm's animals as she made her rounds of the horses. As they talked about Jasmine's adventures, Mike walked up to the group. "We were just talking about your clever case of the missing cat," Mr. Randall said.

Mike looked a little embarrassed, but quickly recovered and took a Sherlock Holmes pose, pretending to hold the famous pipe. "Elementary, my dear Watson." The group all laughed, thinking of how Mike had solved the mystery of Jasmine the cat by making believe he was the famous detective. He told everyone that the celebrated detective Sherlock Holmes would look at every single clue, no matter how insignificant it appeared. He kept everyone smiling with his imitations and quotes from Holmes.

"Seems everyone is here now," Mr. Randall said, "so we'll look at the schedule, and then there will be plenty of time to fill everyone in about what has happened. I think there is another mystery to be solved, and I'm sure that will interest Mike." He held up a chart with the scheduled classes and activities. "Here is a copy for each of you." Mr. Randall passed out a packet of sheets. "You'll find several pages behind the schedule that give you some information about the content of the classes. This session you will continue to work on equestrian skills and longe work. Remember—in the mornings all the staff and the continuing students will meet for practice on the longe line, so that we learn to train not only the horses but the riders as well." Students learned to ride without using their hands and sometimes rode without stirrups. He paused and looked around at the group, who looked at their schedules. "Our senior students will meet us later at dinner. I think you'll be happy to know that CC and Karl passed their teaching requirements—besides being good teachers they also had hardworking students."

The group let out a happy cheer in approval. They had been nervous during the testing because they didn't want to make mistakes for their teachers. When the older students were tested on their ability to teach riding skills, the new students were their pupils. Mr. Randall beamed at the four of them. "You can get settled into your cabins and we'll see you back here for dinner. Any questions?" He waited to see if anyone would respond, but he could see the group was excited to catch up with the latest news and go to their cabins. "Okay, good to see you all and we'll continue later at dinner."

As the other groups all broke up one at a time, the students moved off to settle in and talk to one another.

"We'll catch up with you later at dinner," Cassie called to their friends as she and Annie headed to their small cabin overlooking the main pasture. "I wonder how Got Carrots and the mare are doing. I can hardly wait to see them. And I wonder what Mr. Randall meant by a … mystery." They quickly dropped off their bags and headed to the dining hall.

CHAPTER 8
Trail Ride Plans

Trail Ride Announced

All the students slowly returned to the dining hall and formed their groups around their usual table for dinner. There were additional tables for the parents and guests who visited the students for the first day. This first meeting was always a jovial, happy time as the students and their friends gathered. It was also a chance for the parents and adult sponsors to be included in the plans for the upcoming session. There was much lively discussion in the room as Mrs. R stepped up to the place where she gave announcements and talked about future events. Tonight there was much anticipation about the planned spring outing. She was the head of the riding center and planned all the events and scheduled lessons. A hush fell over the room, and students leaned forward to hear every word. Mrs. R was called that for short because her name was so long that no one could pronounce it, much less remember it. She claimed it was one of the longest names in her native language.

"You may already know," began Mrs. R, "that each young student holiday training session has a special outing activity planned to help all of our students become more proficient and accomplished equestrians. During our last outing during the winter vacation we were lucky to have beautiful, sunny, snowy days for the sleigh rides." She looked around the room at the happy nodding heads. There was a low murmur of whispering voices as the students commented about how much fun it was to not only go on the large sleighs but also practice in the snow with their special driving carts. The driving carts could have mental runners placed over the wheels so they could be driven in snow.

"This spring vacation," she continued, "we have a special outing planned for a trail ride into the area that borders our farm. There are also several neighboring farms and the open land where the wild horses roam. There is an old trail that leads along this beautiful area." There was an appreciative murmur from the audience. She continued, "We'll stay overnight at a campsite along the trail." She paused and looked around the room at the faces of happy anticipation.

For the next few minutes there was a buzzing of animated conversation as the group thought about the excitement of going with the horses on an overnight camping trip. Finally Mrs. R spoke over the low hum of voices. "An important part of the trip planning will be covered in your regular classes and we will have some special meetings. Each of the teams will plan for what they need, since we will be away from the farm for several nights. Our regular trucks will go on ahead with the food for us and the horses, and also take any of the larger items we'll need."

Again there was polite low conversation as the group excitedly took in the details of the upcoming trip. "Our trip will end up at a local farm at the end of the valley where many of you have seen the wild horses," Mrs. R continued. "We'll have some fun events planned when we reach the other farm. The farm called Lost Valley will also have some equestrian visitors from a nearby riding club. There will be a trail riding class that will prepare all of you to handle some of the different surprises that a rider might find on the open trail." She paused and looked at the expectant faces as they leaned forward to hear all the details. There were some whispers among the group as they waited for Mrs. R to continue. "Besides continuing with all your previous riding skills, we have included lessons to practice the skills that will be used in a schooling trail class competition." Mrs. R nodded toward Alex, who was waving his hand in the air. "Yes, Alex, what can we tell you?"

"Will we be practicing for the competition during our regular classes?"

"Oh, most certainly," replied Mrs. R. "In fact when I hand out the schedule, you will see that all the new things that you're going to learn about trail riding are exactly the practice you'll need to do this fun trail class competition. It all works together. All the things you're going to learn for the trail ride and how to be safe with your mounts will be the same things that are in the fun trail class competition." She handed out a sheet of paper that listed all the classes.

Mr. Randall stood up, and Mrs. R nodded to him to add some more information. "Now don't you students worry … you've already mastered the carriages, and riding on the longe line without holding reins or using stirrups. This work will be an easy addition to all the wonderful equestrian skills you have mastered." He assured the students that they were ready for this next adventure. "We're going to have all the older students and several of the instructors, so there will be plenty of help. The trucks will meet us each evening where we stop, so we won't have to carry much on the horses. The trail is a very old, well-worn path that runs the length of the valley. The farms along this open area have used this trail for many years.

"We'll take a small lunch with us." Mr. Randall could see that Alex was concerned that they wouldn't get anything to eat while riding during the day. "The saddles all have a small square leather lunch bag that attaches to the side to carry a light midday snack. That will hold everyone over until the larger meal in the evening." There was a murmur of appreciation and excitement as the campers looked forward to this overnight trip.

Everyone was eager to hear the details of the upcoming trail ride. This was a big step for many of the young riders who only a year earlier would never have thought about learning so much about horses. From the beginning riding lessons on the longe line, including vaulting, to independently riding horses in the arena to driving small carriages, and now being able to ride their own horse across the countryside, was fantastic. They had also learned all the skills necessary to take care of their horses. Annie and Cassie had spent time helping care for the lost filly Got Carrots during the necessary daily horse care routine. It had been touch and go when she had been brought to the stable. They didn't think that she would survive after being alone without the herd for protection and food.

Each student had a notebook with the schedules and classes for this spring session. Mrs. R outlined the program and finished by telling everyone that there would be plenty of time in their first group meeting to go over everything and ask questions. The students automatically began to perform their usual cleaning up after the evening meal in preparation for next morning's breakfast. There was much conversation with all the visitors and new students. The new students had formed a group and were getting their room assignments. Cassie, Annie, Mike, and Alex now felt as if they were old-timers since this would be their third session at Rolling Hills.

Alex turned and said, "I feel as if I'm an old-timer." Everyone looked at Alex making a serious face and then laughed at his funny comment.

"Yes, and we're going to have you help some of the new students find their way around," Mr. Randall said. He thought this was a perfect way for the group to explain and practice their skills. "After all, you may return and begin the instructor's program."

The foursome beamed with the thought of becoming more involved with some part of the wide range of equestrian professions.

"We'll be talking more about equestrian careers during our classes. It has many wonderful opportunities," said Mr. Randall.

Cassie and Annie looked at each other. The girls turned to Mr. Randall and Cassie asked, "Is there a little time to walk through the stable with our folks before they have to leave?"

He glanced at his watch and smiled, "Of course, but make sure you're back in your cabin in time. You need a good night's sleep for tomorrow." He winked.

The girls turned and started the group of visitors off for a quick visit to the stable.

"Wow, I can hardly wait to see our rescued filly, Got Carrots," Cassie said. "I wonder how big she has grown—it's been several months since we last saw her."

Visit to the Horses

Annie and Cassie walked the route they now knew by heart, followed by the adults. They turned the corner to the stalls that housed horses that needed special attention. This area was close to Miss Katy's office so she could have a view of their stalls. The horses heard their footsteps and called one in a regular horse sound and the other with a cute little high-pitched nicker. Both the filly and the newly named, Mystery Mare, were in their same stalls. The only change was that a horse that had been treated for a cut was back in his normal stall. Only the filly and the mare occupied the special attention section of the barn. The rest of the horses were stabled on the main corridor off the big arena.

Cassie and Annie had found the lost filly during their first outing at Rolling Hills. a picnic at the edge of the farm where the wild horses often grazed and came to drink at a nearby lake. While the other students were on a scavenger hunt, Karl and Annie had found what looked like a pile of old rags but turned out to be a half-dead foal.

Luckily for the tiny foal, they had been able to send the truck down to the campsite and drive her back to the center. Miss Katy had helped stabilize her until they could get a veterinarian's care. Annie and Cassie became members of the team providing round-the-clock care that pulled the foal back to health to become a healthy filly.

The next surprise came when Annie and Cassie took a cross-country flight with Annie's parents to view the wild horses. When they landed the small plane on a dirt strip and walked to see the wild horses, they found them at the edge of the farm, but to their dismay they also discovered an injured mare.

They notified the farm owners, who had been able to bring one of their heavy-duty horse transports to pick up the mare. The big surprise was that the mare didn't seem afraid of all the people trying to help her and had walked easily into the horse transport vehicle. They were all amazed that a wild horse didn't seem to be frightened. Perhaps it was because of the shock of the injury, but the biggest surprise was yet to come.

Cassie, Annie, and their family members were surprised to see how much the filly had grown. She appeared to remember them and nickered softly. She had a sweet face with big eyes that followed everything that was happening. After everyone had been shown around and all the animals had been checked, it was time for Annie's parents and Aunt Emma to leave. All the hugs and goodbyes were completed, and the girls waved as the car turned down the driveway.

As the girls walked to their cabin, Annie mused, "You know, that is still the strangest thing about our little filly ... and the Mystery Mare."

CHAPTER 9
Preparation for the Trail Ride

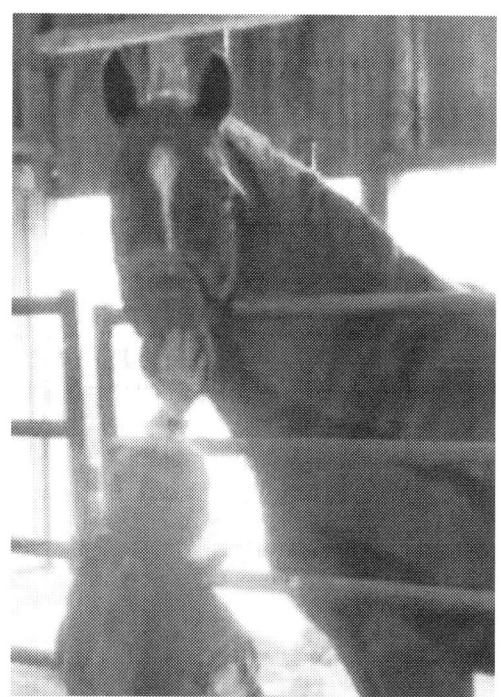

Riding Schedules

There was much excitement as the all the riding groups assembled the next morning in the large hall for breakfast. Mr. Randall looked around the table and saw that everyone in his class was present, so he passed around a sheet of paper that listed the schedule for classes and the overnight trail ride. He began to explain where they would meet next to begin this spring class for students. "For this session everyone will be assigned a horse for the trail riding classes … similar to what we did during the driving lessons." Mr. Randall quickly reviewed the two-week schedule of classes. Since the group had already completed two other riding programs, they knew about the rules and basic routines of the school. He could see by the anticipation on their faces that they wanted to hear about the trail ride. "So if there are no questions …" He paused. "I know you want to hear all about the trail ride."

There was a restrained but enthusiastic response, so Mr. Randall continued. "The trail ride, as many of you already know, will start on the path below our farm. Many of you remember we have a picnic area near the lake where many of the wild horses often come for water." He looked at Annie and Cassie. "That's the area where we had our scavenger hunt and you found the little foal that had apparently become separated from her herd, during a flash flood. Part of the old trail that runs the length of this valley begins there. This old trail is well worn and has been used to travel between the farms in this area. The farm we will visit is called Lost Valley." He waited, as there was an exchange of quiet comments. "It's a very good opportunity for a first overnight trail ride because there are no difficult terrains for the horses and there is a cabin with corrals at about the halfway point. We can easily overnight at this established campground and have a safe place for the horses." Now several students had questions.

"How will we carry something to eat?" Alex asked. The group laughed, because Alex was always interested in the menu.

Mr. Randall smiled his happy smile and continued with the details of the trip. "Everyone will pack one small bag that will have your sleeping bag and small articles for overnight. These bags will be loaded into the trucks that will accompany us with our supplies. You will pick up your picnic lunch from the kitchen before we go to the stables to prepare the horses. As soon as we are all finished tacking the horses, we will walk them to the outside riding arena to assemble and meet up with the rest of the groups." The group was carefully listening as he continued to describe the area. "The campground, where we'll stay, is on this beautiful trail that leads to the ranch we're going to visit. It has small paddocks where the horses may safely overnight. The staff will have set up tents and taken your bedroll and things out to the area with our farm trucks. There is also a small old cabin at the campgrounds, but we will have our things we need brought by the truck." He paused and looked around at the attentive faces. "Are there more questions?"

Where Are the Wild Horses?

There was a long silence and then Mike asked, "Do you think we'll see the wild horses?"

"I guess that depends on where the head stallion is leading the herd," Mr. Randall said. "The herd travels quite an extensive range, depending on the weather and grazing. As you remember, Annie helped find our rescued filly in this area. So it will be interesting to see if the herd is following their normal route. Cassie and Annie took care of the filly and brought her back to good health." He smiled in the direction of Annie and Cassie, who looked a little embarrassed at the attention. "You remember the rest of the story of how they took a flying trip to see the wild horses and discovered that one of them was in need of help. They alerted the farm, and a horse trailer from Rolling Hills picked up the horse and brought it here for medical attention. This turned out to be an amazing coincidence, as the two horses seemed to know each other. The coincidence is indeed strange. No doubt we may find out more about these two interesting horses."

"Mr. Randall," Mike waved his hand to interrupt. Mr. Randall stopped and acknowledged Mike with his knowing smile. "Mr. Randall, do you think we'll discover where these two horses came from?"

"Well," he said thoughtfully. "We do know that the two horses seem to know each other ... sounds like a real mystery doesn't it?"

Mike was already thinking about solving this mystery. "I think we have to find out about the wild herd and where those horses came from. Obviously there are some missing facts."

Mr. Randall noticed that there was a real interest in the wild horses. "This trip should provide us with a perfect opportunity to find out more about the wild horses. The farm we'll visit may have some more information about this herd, because the horses often migrate along this valley, spending grazing time near their horses' fields." He looked around at the group and saw many curious faces. "We'll talk more on this trip, so if there aren't any more questions … we should get ready for the day's classes." He glanced at his watch but didn't need to say another word. The students were gathering their things and hurrying off to get ready for their classes.

Each team of the younger students was made up of four members. Annie, Cassie, Mike, and Alex had been together in the riding program since they started. Some of the other groups didn't have students who stayed continually with the program. This foursome had moved through all the levels of learning, including stable management, horse care, and the riding disciplines. All four had practiced the various riding skills and were now able to go on this overnight ride to a neighboring farm. The students who had progressed this far were very excited because all of their hard work was paying off and they were ready to take a horse on an overnight trail ride with all the responsibility for the special tasks.

CHAPTER 10
Jasmine Does It Again

Jasmine Missing

"Has anyone seen Jasmine?" Cassie walked around the office where the cat loved to hang out, sitting on top of one of the older computers. She checked Jasmine's food bowl, but it looked as if nothing had been touched. She walked down the row of horse stalls, asking the other students who were busy preparing horses, if they'd seen Jasmine lately, but none of the students or barn managers could remember seeing her for at least a day.

When the group assembled at lunch, Cassie said, "I checked with the riders in the main stable and asked them if they had seen Jasmine, but nobody has reported seeing her." Cassie looked worried about her friend. She remembered her first visit to the school when they had stayed in the little cabin. They had heard a sound and upon investigation found a hungry kitten. They had gained her confidence with a dish of cat food. When no owner was found, Jasmine became a cheerful, energetic member of Rolling Hills.

"Did you check her food bowl?" asked Mike. He remembered the last time Jasmine had been missing and her food bowl was untouched. When Jasmine was missing it was Mike's sleuthing techniques that led the group to the old barn. Jasmine loved to climb about and often had everyone cringing in fright at her high acrobatics. She had finally gotten herself stranded high up in the old barn used for hay storage. A group led by Mike, finally found her at the top of the old barn, and she had been rescued. Everyone was relieved, and Jasmine had stayed by Miss Katy's office near the quarantine barn. It seemed she was off again, doing her exploration act.

"Her bowl hasn't been touched, and you know how much she likes eating," answered Cassie in a worried tone. "I took a quick look around in her favorite places and asked everyone to keep a lookout …" She paused and continued, "I sure hope she hasn't gotten herself into trouble again."

"We'll just have to find her again," said Annie, who had been quiet up to this point in the conversation. "We can do the same thing as before and systematically go through all the places she would go, including the old barn." Annie was always thinking ahead with a plan.

The old barn and silo were the remnants of the original farm that had included dairy cows. The barn was more than a hundred years old, with huge, dark timbers that reached up into the wooden roof, now covered with metal. It was important to the farm, because it held all the hay needed to feed the horses.

At the mention of the old barn, Cassie shuddered, remembering how creepy the place was in the dark. The old barn was for hay and feed storage, so it didn't have the big bright lights that were needed on the rest of the farm where the school horses resided. Several stalls on the far end were used to stable the farm staff horses. That section had bright lights, but the other side of the barn where the hay was stored reached high into dark, unseen rafters. This hayloft was one of Jasmine's favorite places to roam and play. Often there were birds nestling in the high rafters, and Jasmine loved to see how close she could get to them. She also enjoyed visiting the horses, walking around the top edge of their stalls, getting nuzzled by their soft noses. Cassie thought about all the strange sounds and said, "I sure hope she's not in that old barn!"

"Don't worry," said Mike. "We won't go when it's dark. After we finish lunch, we'll have a little time before the lessons start and can check the old barn while it's still daylight."

The group went the short distance to the barn, which was right next to the main riding hall and horse stalls. They walked in, and the horses at the far end all called, thinking someone was bringing food.

"They're all talking to us," said Annie as she walked over to the horses and offered them carrots. Miss Katy's beautiful stallion was there and eagerly stretched his neck, looking for a carrot.

They all walked around the barn calling for Jasmine, but after fifteen minutes, Annie called to the group, "Hey, look at the time … we need to get to our lessons."

The group reluctantly left the old barn. They talked about what might have happened to Jasmine and where she might be. They quickly headed over to the main stables to get their horses ready for the afternoon classes. There was much excitement because they were going to meet in the outside arena for the day's lesson.

Riding Lesson

The horses were all cleaned and tacked. The students walked their mounts outside to the arena where the class lined up, each student standing next to a horse. Mr. Randall was already there and gave the command to mount. Shortly the horses were walking around the arena in an organized line. It was a lovely day for riding outside. This class was getting each rider prepared to ride in a group with other horses.

Everyone was mounted and waited for the lesson to begin. Mr. Randall started by reviewing the previous lessons and introducing today's lesson. Each rider was riding the assigned horse for the trail ride so they could get acquainted with their mounts. Cassie was extremely happy, because she had the horse named Little Pony. She remembered how easy he was when she made a mistake, and felt confident that they were a team once again.

Mr. Randall gave the order for the horses to proceed single file to the edge of the arena at the walk. He explained that during the trail ride, the horses would follow in a single line just the way they were practicing, especially when the trail was narrow. During other times they would go in pairs with two horses side by side. He gave the command for the riders to count off by twos. "Ready … all the number two riders move up next to the horse in front of you on the left side." The horses all proceeded in pairs, walking around the arena until he gave the command for the number two riders to move back to single file. The lessons continued for the remainder of the time, with the horses moving into various combinations so that the riders would feel comfortable while on the trail. The command was given for the horses to halt. All the horses halted obediently. Little Pony, however, continued walking and decided that he should join another horse.

"Oh dear," Cassie called out. "I don't seem to be able to get Little Pony to stop."

"Ask him to walk on," directed Mr. Randall. "Ask him again to halt."

The group all stayed quietly at the halt while Cassie asked Little Pony to halt. This time he halted perfectly and Mr. Randall called, "Well done, Cassie." He addressed the class: "You all did a great job at keeping your horses quiet while Cassie got Little Pony to pay attention. This is very important, because if one of the horses becomes confused when we are on the trail ride, it's important for everyone to keep their horse remaining quiet." He looked around at all the attentive faces. "Okay, students … prepare to form a line side by side to dismount your horse, starting with Alex, and then prepare to dismount on my signal." The horses walked around the arena and turned to face Mr. Randall, who stood in the center. The group dismounted and walked the horses back to the main barn to be groomed and placed back in their stalls.

After the students groomed the horses, they met over at the dining hall to talk about preparation for the trip. "Well," said Mr. Randall with his usual happy look, "everyone is doing really well. The reason we practice doing all these changes of pace is because when we're actually riding on the trail, the horses may see something that distracts them. It's important that everyone pays attention to the other riders and horses just like you did in this lesson. In the next lessons we'll continue to practice doing different exercises and changing positions of the horses so they get used to not seeing the same horse alongside. We want the horses to concentrate on your directions and not think about being with their horse buddies." The group laughed at the last comment because they knew certain horses enjoyed being first.

Mr. Randall looked around the group to see if anyone had questions and then continued reviewing the trip schedule. He could see all the expressions of anticipation. "Remember the trucks will bring most of what we need so we don't have to carry much on the horses — you'll all have your snack and water container that straps to the saddle. For tomorrow's lesson, we'll walk the horses from the practice arena where we were today and then ride to the picnic area. We can practice our lesson on this part of the short farm trail to the lake."

There was a murmur as the anticipation for the trip was discussed. The students wondered what the countryside looked like beyond the lower farm area where they had enjoyed picnics and fun activities. There was much speculation about the wild horses and whether they would see any other animals along the trail.

At this comment Cassie said, "What other animals?"

The rest of the group heard her quavering voice and immediately assured her that they would be safe from strange animals. Mr. Randall knew the area well and would make sure they were protected.

Chapter 11
Jasmine Gets Into Trouble

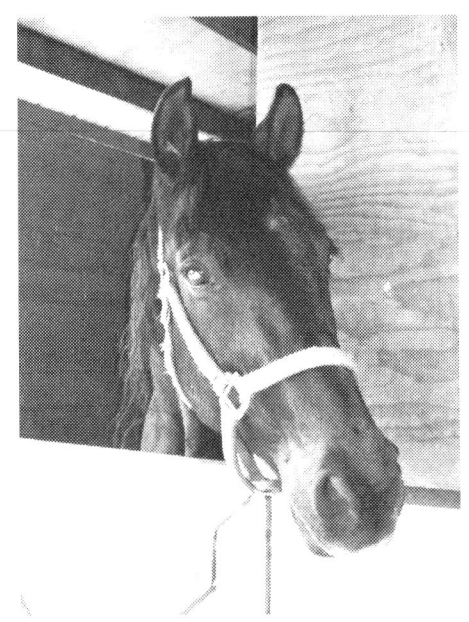

Where Is Jasmine?

Jasmine had been absent from the barn scene for what seemed like a long period of time. The groups spent many days practicing trail riding skills and preparing for the overnight ride with the horses. The campers made a list of the items needed for the trip. Even though the trucks would meet the group each evening carrying the large items, each camper carried needed items. Each camper had been provided with a basic list and then added small items. Anything not going on the truck had to fit into the small container that was carried on the saddle.

The campers were concentrating on the preparation when Alex said, "Has anyone seen Jasmine?"

"I heard that Miss Katy walked around looking for her, but no one has seen her," murmured Cassie. "I'm really worried. Maybe something has happened. You know how she loves to explore ... especially high places."

"She's probably gone off to hunt and check out new places," said Annie. But then she doubted what she had said and added, "You know, she doesn't miss too many meals."

Mike stood looking around, trying to think where Jasmine would go. "We should try again and walk around the old barn, because that's where she likes to go for adventure, checking out the birds. There is a short break before the next session."

The foursome headed over to the older barn again, with Cassie following slowly in the rear. She didn't like the old barn because it had dark corners on the side where the hay was stacked. She remembered the last time the group had spent hours looking for Jasmine, and now, here they all were again, looking for her. The opposite side was brightly lighted because there were several stalls where the private horses were housed. They turned on the luminous overhead lights and decided to separate to cover most of the barn. The four horses stalled in the old barn began to call, believing that it was mealtime. Annie and Cassie walked over and gave each one of them a carrot so they wouldn't feel slighted. The group remembered the last time that Jasmine had ended up at the very top of the old barn and couldn't get back down the ladder she had climbed. She loved climbing up on the top edge of the stalls and had scared everyone with her acrobatic antics. They all secretly worried that Jasmine had gotten herself into another dangerous situation since she loved high places. They were walking around calling her when a muted sound was heard near the horse stalls.

"Over here," called Cassie. "Over here ... I think it might be Jasmine."

The four immediately walked around the stall that had been built into the old barn. There was a space between the old barn walls and the wall of the newly constructed stall.

As the group walked around the stall area, they could hear the faint sound of a cat.

"It sounds as if it's in the stall," said Alex excitedly.

The group began to walk around the stalls to see if they could hear it more clearly. It sounded muffled and very weak. "I wonder if she has slipped into the space between the stall and the barn wall," said Mike. He always approached problems as if they were a mystery.

Alex stopped near the wall and placed his ear against it. "Hey, I think I hear something."

The other three immediately came over to Alex to see if they could hear the sounds. They all stood absolutely quiet for what seemed a long time. All of a sudden they heard a small, soft cry. "Jasmine!" the group said in unison.

"She sounds as if she is behind the wall," said Cassie.

"Yes, I think you're right," said Alex. "We have to get some help. Someone should stay here, and someone should go back to the main barn and find Mr. Randall or Miss Katy."

"You all stay here, and I'll go and try to find Mr. Randall … I think I know where he is," said Annie.

Jasmine in Trouble

They all looked at her and nodded agreement. Annie ran back over to the barn, and as luck would have it, she ran into both Mr. Randall and Miss Katy. He was just checking about some of the trip details. They both looked up as Annie hastily walked up to them. They sensed her urgency. She quickly relayed her mission. "We have found Jasmine … she seems to have fallen behind a wall in the old barn."

As the three hurriedly returned to the old barn, Karl saw them and called, "Do you need some help?"

Karl joined the mission because it seemed they might need every hand. Quickly they followed Annie back to the old barn and stood listening to figure out where the sound was coming from. Mr. Randall leaned down and put his ear to the wall. He stood up and announced that indeed it sounded like a cat behind the stall wall panel.

"What should we do, Mr. Randall?" said Alex.

"I think we have an easy solution with Miss Katy's help." He turned to Miss Katy. "Since I think she is in the space between the stall and the barn wall, will you go into your stallion's stall so he isn't frightened while I take part of the wall away?"

The inside stall wall was made with interlocking pieces of wood that were not nailed to anything but slipped one on top of the other and locked in place along a metal track on each side. Mr. Randall started to remove several of the wall slats to see if he could see her. Miss Katy went into her horse's stall while Mr. Randall started to remove the wooden slats of the stall wall carefully, one piece at a time. Everyone hardly breathed while Alex pointed a flashlight into the dark space between the stall's wooden side and the barn wall. After Mr. Randall had removed several slats, the group staring into the dark sighed in relief. The flashlight shone along the inside of the dark wall and suddenly revealed … "There she is," said Alex. Jasmine was huddled in the space between the two walls. "Oh dear, she doesn't look good."

She didn't move as the flashlight outlined her crouched form. They recognized her tabby coloring. Mr. Randall and Karl positioned themselves on either end and carefully removed each remaining wooden slat until they could reach her. Mr. Randall extended his arms down into the space and carefully lifted her out.

"Let's see if we can cautiously slip these stall slats back in the track so Miss Katy's stallion can safely walk around. He seems a little worried about what's going on in his stall," said Karl as he helped replace the partition while Miss Katy stood with her horse. He seemed calm, as though nothing unusual was happening, because his owner was there. The students quickly completed the work, and Jasmine was gently carried back to Miss Katy's office so her injuries could be examined.

Everyone stood at the edge of Miss Katy's office anxiously watching while Jasmine was placed on a blanket. She looked very weak and didn't try to move. Miss Katy carefully looked to see if she had serious cuts that might be bleeding. She looked up and told the group that it didn't appear that Jasmine had any noticeable serious injuries, but she was going to need a thorough veterinary check. She cautioned the worried students that if Jasmine fell into this wall space from a distance, she might have serious internal injuries.

Almost on cue the anxiously watching group sighed ... a sound of relief.

Miss Katy spoke first "I'm going to take Jasmine to the veterinary hospital right now, because if there is something more serious, she may need immediate attention.

"Let's hope for the best," said Miss Katy as she gently wrapped Jasmine with the blanket and placed her in the sturdy animal carrier so she wouldn't have to move her any more than necessary. "I'll let you know as soon as I return how things are progressing." With a knowing look, and a glance to Mr. Randall and Karl, she added, "Now, you have lots to think about with your camping trip, and we're going to get Jasmine the best help available."

The group trailed Miss Katy to her car to see her on her way. They then slowly walked back to the hall where dinner was already being served. The campers were quiet as they sat down at their assigned table and waited their turn to go through the serving line. Mr. Randall understood how worried they were and started talking about the upcoming trip. "I know how worried everyone is about Jasmine, but Miss Katy will do the best she can—our veterinary clinic is one of the best, so she is in good hands."

Annie was the first to reply. "We're lucky we found her before she was there any longer."

"Yes," replied Mr. Randall, "that's a positive note, because it would be more serious if she had been there too long without water. We can hope that since she didn't look too hurt with any cuts, that there should be a good outcome."

The students looked around at one another, and there was a faint look of relief upon hearing Mr. Randall's words. "So now on an optimistic note, we'll all think positively about Jasmine, knowing that she is getting the best care." Noticing that the group seemed happier, he decided to change the subject. He handed around some small notebooks.

Trail Ride Checklist

"What's this?" asked Mike.

"This is a checklist." He turned his attention to Annie and Cassie. "You both know what this is."

They both looked surprised, but Cassie's face brightened and she said, "Yes, it's a checklist just like the ones we use when we fly to make sure we haven't forgotten to do something important. When it's important not to forget something, a checklist is a way to remember a series or a list of important items. Often the list is outlined in the order of importance."

Mike jumped into the conversation. "When we were getting the carriages ready there were things that had to be done before other things … they had to be done in correct order. You couldn't put the carriage to the horse if the horse didn't have any harness!"

The group laughed, thinking of how strange that would be.

"Good," Mr. Randall said. "So now you have your checklists for the trip. Everyone should take a good look at the list so that when we discuss the different items, you can ask questions." He looked around to see if there were any questions. "It's our turn," he said, and he stood, motioning the group to follow him through the dinner serving line.

"Oh boy, my favorite," said Alex. "Spaghetti with meatballs."

The group was happily talking about the upcoming trip, and the stress about Jasmine seemed to be lessened. The time flew by, and before long, the table had been cleaned and the food trays returned. They were suddenly aware that Miss Katy was approaching the table. There was an abrupt silence as she sat down. They hung on her every word.

CHAPTER 12
Got Carrots Has a Lesson

New Lesson for Got Carrots

The girls went to Miss Katy's office because they were going to start to work with Got Carrots and begin her new lesson. She had already learned how to stand and have her halter put on, so it was time to advance the lessons. It was unusual not to see Jasmine sitting on top of

Miss Katy's older computer monitor with its large back—she loved the flat top and the warmth. It was a perfect perch. In fact, Miss Katy hadn't replaced it because it worked and Jasmine loved it. We are strangely happily habituated to many things in life that animals often satisfy by their funny behaviors.

They were now standing in front of Got Carrots's stall, and Miss Katy had her halter in her hand. "The filly is very good at wearing her halter since you last worked with her. Several of the older resident students came by each day and practiced with her. She is a very quick learner and has an agreeable personality." Miss Katy proceeded to open the stall door and stood next to Got Carrots. Got Carrots immediately stood at attention in anticipation. She knew several cues and understood that if she performed her tasks, she would receive a carrot.

"She hasn't forgotten," murmured Cassie.

"She is so attentive to the commands," said Annie.

"Now we'll walk her to the outside paddock where she is normally turned out." Miss Katy opened the large door in the stall that led to an outside fenced area. She stopped at the door and gave the command to halt. Got Carrots stopped at the door and waited. Now Miss Katy told her to walk on. They walked to the end to the fence and halted. This time Miss Katy patted her on the shoulder and gave her a carrot. "Okay, now it's your turn." And she handed the lead line to Cassie.

Cassie's eyes opened wide. Miss Katy saw that she felt uncertain and said, "You take the lead line and give the command, and I'll walk by your side in case you need help."

Cassie looked confident, took the lead line, and gave the command: "Walk on."

Halter Class Practice

The lesson went very well, and Miss Katy explained that there are halter competition classes in which young horses demonstrate obedience to commands on the halter. "These are often performed on a triangle marked course," she said. "You both did very well with the filly, so we should see how we could fit some practice between your regular lessons. We're going to have a halter class to help the older students prepare their horses in training." Both girls looked very pleased. "I see it's time for your next class, so we'll get together soon and make a schedule."

Horse breeders often test the quality of their horses by completing a halter class. The classes may be judged on conformation and grooming, but behavior is considered, too. Horses are asked to stand, walk, and trot in various patterns, depending on the rules for that particular sport horse. The students practice so that when they take their horses in training to a show, they will have had an opportunity to practice at a schooling show.

The girls fairly floated down the corridor by the main stalls and into the main area and settled down on the bleachers where their class was meeting. The classes often met in the arena, especially if there was a horse demonstration. Today the arena was set up for a trail class competition. There were poles on the ground, cones in various positions, and an outline of a box.

Mr. Randall was in the arena talking to Karl, who was sitting on his favorite horse, BBH. The three letters were short for Big Black Horse. Karl occasionally competed with this energetic, semiretired jumper. In fact the last time there had been a jumping competition at Rolling Hills, Karl didn't win the contest, even though he rode a clean round. The students discovered the reason why he wouldn't push BBH faster to win the timed event. BBH had suffered a leg injury while jumping when he was younger and had been given to the Rolling Hills farm to rest and slowly recuperate. This meant he could be lightly ridden in small events but not at the previously fast pace. So BBH did a perfect round with Karl but placed second because he was too slow. That was just fine for Karl.

Mr. Randall walked over to the edge of the arena where the class was sitting. "Glad to see you're all ready for the trail class. Karl is riding BBH and is going to walk through the various parts of the class. We have trail classes to practice in a quiet place to accustom the horse to new objects before we ride in unknown places. It's to build confidence for both the rider and horse. Let's watch Karl walk through the pattern, and then we'll have him do it again and talk about each part of the exercise."

The groups watched as Karl began to walk over the uneven poles on the ground and continued to weave through a series of tall cones. The exercise was going well, and Karl arrived at the box that was a series of poles lying on the ground to form a box. He stepped into the box. After BBH stood perfectly still, Karl gave the command to step out. The next task was to sidestep to pick up a latch on the gate. BBH did very well, moving effortlessly sideways because he knew many basic dressage commands. Karl now moved him away from the wall and walked over to where Mr. Randall was standing.

Alex had his hand raised and Mr. Randall nodded to him. "How did Karl make him move sideways?"

"Yes, that is the one of the exercises we haven't covered. Karl is preparing for the advanced trail class, so a few of the exercises are not required at beginning levels. Let's watch Karl again and see what commands he gives to BBH."

The group watched as Karl again brought BBH to a halt and then had him move sideways. "I see," called out Alex. "Karl is gently tapping BBH on his side."

"Yes, very good, Alex, that you could see that very small motion. It's not the force that makes the horse move sideways, but the fact that the horse has learned a cue or signal from the rider. In our next riding lessons we will begin to learn advanced rider signals that let us not only tell our mounts to walk forward and stop but also move in other directions."

CHAPTER 13
The Trail Ride

Day of the Trail Ride

The day of the trail outing finally arrived. Everyone had gathered and organized their belongings, performing all the tasks as practiced, and the horses were all assembled in the large outdoor riding arena waiting to leave. There was excitement among the group as they waited for the command to form a line. Finally the instructors took their position among the students, and the trail ride had begun. Although this part of the farm was known to many of the students, this was the first time the younger ones had ridden any distance and past the lower picnic area. Their destination was at the lower edge of the pasture near a small lake where the wild horses often came to drink and find food that was put out by the farm team when grazing was difficult. The group had a glorious ride through the picturesque countryside beyond the farm.

The riders were now walking slowly along a wide trail that ran over the lower edge of a series of small hills to their right. The area was a wonderful, large grassy expanse that continued as far as they could see. After several hours of walking through the beautiful green fields that neighbored the farm, the younger students were excited to see all the expanse of the farm that stretched out for miles

The group enjoyed the beautiful green countryside. The pace was slow, and everyone had a chance to look around. There was much interest in and discussion about the wild horses. They had hoped to see them near the trail, because the herd stayed fairly close to the farm. Especially during the winter months when finding food was more difficult, the herd stayed near Rolling Hills. The equestrian farm staff always put out piles of hay at the far ends of the lower pastures near the lake.

At this time of year, as the meadows became lush, the horses had more freedom to roam and find the nourishing grass they had missed during the harsher winter months. Instead of staying around the source of food from the farm, they could roam in many directions and find the best grazing. As the group rode through the countryside, they kept a lookout for the herd. Annie and Cassie were especially interested in seeing the herd again to discover anything that might let them learn more about the rescued horse and the mare.

The path now took a turn and started to narrow along a steeper side of the hills. The horses followed in a single line. Little streams ran on the sides of the trail, part of the runoff from the melting winter snows. They were all quiet running streams, unlike the quick running water that often is the result during a sudden storm.

It was believed that during one of these sudden storms, which the rescued horse had become swept away from the herd. It was during a fun picnic near the edge of Rolling Hills that Annie and Karl found the little foal all huddled in a small form that looked like a pile of rags. The story had a happy ending, and with constant nursing the little horse made a speedy recovery. The running water reminded Annie about how they had found the little horse, and she thought that it would be wonderful to discover more about this wild herd.

Lunch Break

The morning passed quickly, and soon the group was looking for the place where they would have a quick lunch. Mr. Randall held up his arm to signal them to stop. When the horses were all halted, he called, "Right up ahead there is a shady groups of trees where we can stop. Watch me for the command to dismount so we have all the horses calm." The group walked farther toward the clearing, and Mr. Randall gave the order to dismount. "We're all going to stand with our horses for a quick bite to eat and then continue on. Please pay attention to your horse while we eat our sandwiches — it's not their dinnertime yet. Hold onto your reins. Don't let the horses put their heads down to eat, because they could step through the reins. We'll be here about fifteen minutes for this quick break."

Everyone stood in a semicircle so that the horses would not brush up against each other and their heads would all face the same way. The group had practiced safely handling the horses on the ground and on the trail. All the riders had mastered basic skills by practicing in the school arena. They practiced such exercises as stopping and turning, as well as having control at different gaits. They had also practiced what to do in case of an emergency, or if a horse became frightened. So far the trip had been uneventful.

Mr. Randall surveyed the happy group munching on their sandwiches. The conversation was about the trip and the farm they were going to visit. Everyone was looking forward to the events at the farm.

"Okay, everyone, get ready to pack up your things and mount your horse," Mr. Randall said. "Remember that after we mount, everyone will remain at the halt until I give the command to walk on." Mr. Randall waited until the group had put the remaining items away. He looked around and saw that the riders were standing by their horses and awaiting the command to mount. In a loud, clear voice, he said, "Riders, mount your horse." Riders carefully lifted themselves into the saddle and stood waiting for Mr. Randall's next command. The horses obediently stood as if waiting to hear his voice, which they all knew very well. The next command came. "Riders, walk on."

The group wound their way around the little stream that ran beside the trail until they suddenly came to a point where the stream ran across the path. Mr. Randall lifted his arm, signaling to the group, "Riders halt."

The riders all looked around, and suddenly Cassie called, "I see … there's water running across the trail."

"We have all practiced walking in water with the horses on the farm," Mr. Randall said. "This little bit of water running over the trail only makes the ground look darker. I would like each of the older students to pair with one of the younger riders." The group slowly moved the horses into pairs, each with an older rider and a younger student. The pairs had all passed by following each other across the small area of running water.

It was now Cassie and her partner's turn to walk across. Little Pony was always good and obedient, but today he decided that he didn't like the way the water looked. To Little Pony it was different than the water they had walked through on the farm. Mr. Randall noticed and called to the older student, "Get Little Pony close … right next to your horse, and lead him across the water."

The riders all looked on expectantly, and sure enough, Little Pony walked right across the water with Karl, who was riding the other horse. A small quiet cheer went up from the group, and Cassie looked relieved. Karl turned and said, "Cassie, sometimes it takes another horse to take the lead. This has nothing to do with the rider but the fact that horses tend to follow other horses."

"Oh," she said, "That's good to know, because I thought I had done something wrong."

"No, it's not your fault," Karl said, "You stayed very calm … Little Pony knew he didn't need to be frightened. I was once out with a group of riders going over a cross-country preparation for a competition. My mare decided that she wasn't going to go near a small water jump. It wasn't but a few inches deep, but it appeared unusual in its color. Horses often notice small differences in their surroundings as a means of survival and self-protection. After they see it isn't scary, they will normally walk through it. We used another schooled horse to show my horse the water was all right—just like what we did with Little Pony." Cassie looked relieved that someone as experienced as Karl had had the same problem. "An interesting fact about horse vision is that they can see depth almost as well as cats. Some animal books state horses may not be able to see the difference between blue and orange." He paused and looked at Cassie's attentive face and added, "That may make it difficult for horses to judge water, and the reason why we have to train them to become accustomed to crossing a stream."

"Gee, you know so much. How did you learn all those things about horses?"

"Science classes are included as part of the coursework, and I decided to do some reports about how horses see. It may explain in part why some of the obstacles that we ask horses to go near are difficult for them. Little Pony only needed to be distracted and follow my horse."

Now that the group was on the other side of the rivulet, the trail began to broaden and the riders were able to ride in pairs. There was still no sign of the wandering wild herd, but everyone hoped they would see them before they made camp that evening. As they walked along, the riders chatted gaily and told horse stories.

Mr. Randall started to talk about a horse that was being used to transport some of the group's food. "Here we were getting ready to spend the day walking across the beautiful area in southern Spain called the Marismas, in a national park near the river Guadalquivir. This wildlife area is part of the Coto Doñana National Park." The riders, hearing Mr. Randall begin one of his wonderful adventure stories, all tried to get close enough to hear him. "Hang on, people," he called. "We have too many horses too close together. Everyone go back to your partners and I won't say another word about the story until tonight by the campfire."

Happy to hear they hadn't missed any of the tale, the riders regrouped their horses into pairs. Mike, who loved to hear about Mr.

Randall's exciting journeys when he lived in Spain, thought that he would certainly like to travel someday.

The scene began to change, and in the distance an area of trees could be seen. The trail disappeared between the trees, and Mike wondered where it ended. "Mr. Randall," he called. "Are we headed for those trees where the trail seems to go?"

Trail Through the Woods

Mr. Randall called back and asked the riders to pass the information along. The riders were instructed to rearrange themselves into single file and prepare to halt before they rode through a small forest area. The riders did as requested, and Mr. Randall faced the group. He explained that the forest area trail wasn't very wide, but it took too long to go around on the other trail. "We want to make sure we arrive at our camping area with time to spare. Everyone should be extra attentive to the horses. During the day, deer are often running through the woods, taking a shortcut to the grass while staying hidden, just like they do in the pastures at Rolling Hills." He gave the command, "Everyone get ready and walk on."

It was a short distance, and as soon as the riders passed into the trees, they could see where the trail exited to the next open grassland. They were nearing what looked as if it were an open door, when right in front of the lead horse, five deer came leaping and running across the trail. It happened so quickly that no one could believe what had happened. The horses didn't react as much as you might think, because deer often jumped in and out of the pastures back on the farm. Everyone looked around to see where the deer had gone, but they were nowhere to be seen.

Mr. Randall called to the group, "Did you all see the deer?"

Mike, who was at the end of the group said, "What deer!" Everyone laughed.

The riders continued the short way to where the trees opened again into lush green fields. The riders could now spread out into groups of two and three horses, and the view was spectacular. "How much farther until the campground?" a voice called.

"Not too much more," answered Mr. Randall. "In fact, when we reach that curve up ahead, we should all start looking for a small cabin.

The corral for the horses is near the side of the cabin, and our supply truck will meet us there."

Even though the group had experienced a glorious ride through the picturesque countryside, it had seemed long. For many of the younger students, this was one of the longest times they had ridden. One of the older student leaders called, "Everyone keep a sharp eye out and look for the campground. It's at the side of a hill, hidden by trees and large brush. You'll see a small horse corral that looks like the one near our picnic place."

"Gosh," said Cassie. "Do you think we missed it?" She sounded concerned. She was always conscientious and tried her best.

An older student who had made the trip several times assured her that it should be up ahead where they could see that the hill took a slight turn. "It should be right in that protected side just around this bend," he said, pointing.

Cassie, who had been doing extremely well during the flying lessons at spotting small things on the ground, kept looking to see if she could find any small indication. She thought that the wood fences would all blend in—kind of like one of those puzzles where you have to find the hidden objects.

Everyone was busily scanning the sides of the hill, looking for the first hint of the campground. The group kept walking the horses along the obvious trail, and then Cassie called out, "I see the fencing for the horses … I see the corral."

They approached the area, and the outline of the small campsite came into view. Cassie turned in her saddle and teased Mike, "Well, Sherlock, looks like you have an assistant."

"Well done, Watson," he chimed back. Dr. Watson is the famous detective's well-known assistant who helps him solve very difficult cases. He is also the narrator of the detective's stories.

Annie, Cassie, Mike, and Alex had several fun problems to solve together. All four had been taking the holiday riding program and this was the third time they would be together taking classes. They were good friends, and this camping trip was one of the many exciting adventures that the friends participated. Here they were once again taking classes at Rolling Hills … this time it was a trail ride.

CHAPTER 14
The Cabin

Setting Up Camp

The riders continued to turn slightly off the main trail that ran along the valley. Because the trail was narrow, they formed a single line and rode the short distance to where they could see a rustic camp setting with wooden horse corrals and a small cabin farther up the hill.

Mr. Randall, who was leading the riders, called for everyone to stop. "Let me have your attention," he called. The horses all came to a halt so the riders could hear the instructions. Mr. Randall directed them to go to a safe place to dismount, and secure and untack their horses. As soon as all the horses were safely unsaddled, he gave instructions for how they would walk their mounts to the corral. The horses would be given food and water first, and then the campers would begin setting up camp and preparing the evening meal.

There was still some daylight before the evening meal would be ready. The group was curious about the campsite and asked Mr. Randall several questions. They asked if it would be all right if they walked around the area. He replied that they might want to investigate some of the interesting things remaining from previous campers. It was okay to look around as long as they stayed within sight of the campground.

"Can we go and look at the old log cabin on the hill near the horse corrals?" asked Mike. He was always interested in a mystery. "Who lives there?"

"No one lives there," Mr. Randall replied. "It's just a small place for protection in case of a storm. Many of the cowboys would be moving cattle in this area and needed a place to get out of a bad storm. As you remember, last year we had a big unexpected storm pass through the area. It was so bad that it scattered the wild horses. The problem in this area is the unpredictable weather that suddenly changes, so for this reason there are many of these cabins located throughout the area."

"That sounds interesting," said Mike.

"Don't be too long, because dinner should be ready in a little less than an hour."

The foursome walked past the corral where the horses were happily munching, and approached the little log cabin.

"Isn't this the cutest little house?" said Annie. "Wouldn't it be fun to find out who built it and something about the people who stopped by? Sounds like a mystery to me." She directed this comment mostly to Mike.

They walked into the one-room cabin and surveyed the furnishings. It was very plain with only the needed furniture. There were bare wood bunks where a sleeping bag would make for a comfortable night's rest. Toward the middle of the room was a rough finished table with uncomfortable-looking wood chairs. At the far end was an open fireplace where a visitor could make a fire for warmth and cooking.

"Not much here, but this would certainly be better than being out in a storm," pondered Alex.

"You remember that horrible sudden storm last year right before we had our picnic at the edge of the farm? That was pretty bad for the wild herd. It's when that poor little foal that had been washed away in the heavy downpour and separated from the herd was found. This would be a great place if you were out in that storm," commented Mike.

Mike interrupted the conversation, "Hey, look at this!" He was inspecting the walls of the cabin. "These walls have newspaper stuffed in the cracks!"

The only way to keep cold drafts out of old cabins with spaces between the logs was to stuff the cracks with mud or old paper. They walked over to see what Mike had discovered. He had gently lifted out a section of old newspaper and placed it on the wooden table.

"Wow, this looks old." They carefully spread the paper out so they could see the first page with the name and date of the paper. "This is amazing — do you realize how old this is?" They carefully looked through the pages and the strange advertisements. "Let's take this and show it to Mr. Randall. It's almost time for dinner," said Mike."

They carefully folded up the frayed papers to keep them readable. As they walked past the horses, there was much nickering. "They look happy and well-fed," remarked Cassie, who was feeling a bit hungry. "Wonder what they brought in the trucks," she mused.

The trucks carrying the horse feed and camp supplies had already arrived. The campers had quickly helped to unload the larger vans, finding their small tents and sleeping bags. The final preparations for the evening had been made, and each camper had pitched a tent for the night.

The wonderful smell from the chuck wagons wafted through the air. Being outdoors gave everyone an appetite. Soon they heard the familiar sound of the dinner bell. The hungry riders filed past the food trucks and scooped up wonderful-smelling camp food that had been brought by the trucks. With everyone seated around the big fire, an evening of camp food, friends, and song was planned. It was turning into the end of a perfect day with a beautiful sunset and stars beginning to appear in the darkening sky.

Campfire and Music

"Mr. Randall, play some Spanish songs," a voice said. Much to Mr. Randall's surprise, someone handed him his guitar, which had been carried carefully in the van. "Well, I guess I can't say I don't have my guitar." He laughed, picked up the guitar, and began to play.

Mr. Randall had spent several years in Spain as a teacher. There were many wonderful things about Spanish culture, and he had learned to play traditional flamenco music. The strains of the characteristic beats enthralled the group, and soon they began to clap lightly to the syncopated rhythms of Sevillanas.

The music of southern Spain is very popular for traditional dance and festivals. During the spring, each town has a festival that celebrates a favorite saint. There is dancing and clapping to the beat of the captivating sounds of Sevillanas. New music and various dance steps are added or changed each year. Everyone enjoys the fun of being able to join in and learn to clap and dance to the captivating beat.

The group enjoyed the music until Mr. Randall declared, "You all need to get a good night's sleep for a long day tomorrow." The happy although tired students sighed their disappointment but slowly headed off to their tents. A beautiful moon was rising in the hills, and Mr. Randall strummed the last chords to send the riders for much-needed rest.

CHAPTER 15
An Uninvited Guest

Cassie Meets a Critter

Morning shown bright, and the breakfast bell sounded. The smell of bacon and eggs wafted through the camp, and sleepy heads poked out of the tents to greet a bright, sunny morning. The campers helped themselves to plates of the freshly cooked breakfast. Once fortified, they cleaned up and put away the breakfast items and rolled their tents to be stored in the trucks.

Annie and Cassie had finished packing and were headed to get their horses ready when they heard a strange noise coming from one of the trucks.

"What was that?" called Cassie, who was standing closest to the truck and had a wide-eyed expression.

Both stopped to listen. There it was again … a rattling noise. It sounded as if someone was in the truck looking for something. Cassie raised her voice, "Who's in there? Come out and show yourself."

They thought it was the boys playing some kind of trick. They both waited, but nothing happened. "Can you hear anything?" Cassie asked.

Annie shook her head. They stood straining to hear any sound from inside the truck.

When they didn't hear anything, they both turned to leave. Suddenly, Cassie caught sight of a small head peering around a box sitting in the back of the truck. Annie had started walking away, but Cassie stood still, waiting to see what would happen next. A small brown animal walked to the edge of the truck, jumped down, and scurried away.

Cassie jumped back. "Heavens, what was that! Some little brown thing just jumped out of the truck. It moved so quickly."

Annie said, "I didn't even get a look at it."

"What happened?" asked Alex, who had walked up to the truck to see if he could help pack up the belongings.

Mike was right behind him and sensed something interesting happening. "What's up?" He was always interested in a mystery to be solved.

Cassie was nervously shaking her finger and pointing to the truck. "A little brown creature just jumped out of there!"

"What kind of creature?"

"I … I don't know," stammered Cassie. The boys looked to Annie for information, but she shook her head.

Karl, one of the older students walked up to the truck carrying an item to be packed.

"Don't go in there!" shouted Cassie.

"What's going on?" Karl asked.

Cassie suddenly spoke up. "There are creatures in the truck—one just jumped out." She indignantly shook her finger in the direction of the truck.

Karl looked surprised, but calmly assured them that the small creatures running around in the area were probably harmless. "They're only looking for food. Surely they're more afraid of you. Let's see if there are others hiding." He banged the back of the truck. Nothing was seen or heard. "See, no more creatures. They would certainly leave with all that noise."

Cassie whistled a little song. She was still unsure. The group continued packing their belongings into the truck.

"What were those little brown creatures?" Mike asked. He was always curious.

"Oh, they were most likely harmless type of small scavenging animals that are around and wouldn't bother anyone," Karl said. "They're only a nuisance, so it's good you disturbed them before they made a mess in the truck. They're kind of cute when they play together."

Cassie stopped her whistling and wrinkled her nose. "Not much fun when they jump out of nowhere."

"Cassie, you're going to have to get comfortable seeing these creatures. They live here … we're probably going to see plenty more," said Karl to encourage her.

Cassie made a funny face. Karl continued, "You want to get a chance to see nature, don't you?"

"Not that close … and not jumping right in front of me," she replied crossly.

"Okay, let's get going and get our horses ready. We have a whole day of riding before we arrive at Lost Valley," said Karl with mock seriousness.

The foursome scurried off to get their mounts ready. Cassie had already forgotten about the brown creature. They busied themselves brushing and tacking their horses. Soon the group was mounted and the day had begun.

CHAPTER 16
Lost Horse Island

Beautiful Views

The campers were excited and waiting to see what the next part of the trail ride would uncover. The countryside had been mostly meadows interspersed with bands of wooded areas. The trail was easily seen and quite wide. There weren't any difficult places to navigate as might be the case with more advanced trail rides. This trail was a well-worn path. The view opened up into an area of greenery with water. The group walked along at a slow, even pace, enjoying the beautiful view in the distance. Mr. Randall briefed the group about the tiny distant island.

He had everyone's attention and Mike asked, "How did they get the name for the island?"

"Well, it's an interesting story, but long ago this area was inhabited by several different tribes of Indians. Of course they all had horses, but they didn't have a place to keep them safe, especially from other tribes who would take any horses that were roaming free."

"I know what they did," said Cassie. "They used the island as a corral!"

"Yes, you're right," replied Mr. Randall. "The tribes swam the horses over to the island and had their own built-in corral. The grazing was great, so the horses didn't want to swim unless someone was forcing them to leave the island. You can see that's how the name Lost Horse Island came about, because it appeared that the horses had vanished. There are many interesting stories about the history of this area."

The riders looked off into the distance at the beautiful view of greenery and the lake below. The island in the distance didn't appear very large, so the next question came from Annie.

"How large is the island? It doesn't seem very big, and it's very close to the mainland. Cassie and I flew to an island with horses, but it was quite large, with many buildings."

The questions flew fast as everyone wanted to know all about this intriguing island with horses. "Hold your horses: I can answer only one question at a time," Mr. Randall said. "So first, the island is more than two thousand acres. The lake is the largest freshwater body of water west of the Mississippi. The island has been turned into a national park, and there are only a handful of horses on it. There are no buildings, and the island is mostly grassland with some trees. Many tourists take a kayak or a boat launch to visit, so they can walk around and see the view."

"Wow," said Alex, who was very interested in history. "How can we find out more about the island?"

"There are many interesting webpages from the National Parks Department that explain all about the area and the activities. We'll have a wonderful view as we ride along this ridge toward the farm. There are great places for camping and trails for hiking."

The horses walked along at their slow pace while the young people took in the view of grasslands, water, and the island. As the island became nearer, they could see more details. On one side there was a forest of what seemed to be pine trees. On the other side appeared what might be grazing areas for the horses.

"Do you think we'll see any of the wild horses?" called Mike from the back of the line.

"Hopefully we may get lucky. This will be an easier place to spot them, because unlike our wild herd, they can't go very far on the island. The other wild herd of horses has miles and miles to roam between the farms. Actually it's more than the distance we are riding to the farm we're going to visit. This valley extends miles beyond the farm we're visiting. Let's all keep a lookout. There are also many other types of wildlife in this area …"

Mr. Randall didn't get to finish his description because Cassie, who was a little concerned about new "creatures," interrupted. "What kind of wildlife?"

"Nothing to be worried about," he reassured Cassie. "The types of wildlife in this area are more afraid of you. When they hear our horses and voices, they'll stay away."

Cassie signaled her relief by whistling a few bars of her favorite tune. "What should we look for besides the horses on the island?"

"We may see some bighorn sheep and deer like the ones that ran through the forest. Since we're not going to walk through any more forest areas until we reach the farm, we don't have to worry about surprises. The deer normally like to hang at the edge of meadows and forests so they can find protection. There might be some bald eagles … certainly on the lake there should be waterbirds."

The riders were passing the area with the island fairly near on their right. Everyone was looking to see if they could spot the wild horses. Alex had compact binoculars and was scanning the view. The distance between the mainland and the island appeared close from where they rode.

Alex suddenly called out, "I see the horses … they're all grouped together in an open space of the meadow … all grazing."

Mr. Randall called for the group to halt so everyone could concentrate on finding the spot the Alex was describing. They all stood quietly, watching the horses in the distance. They could also see small boats slowly moving near the island. There was one powerboat launch headed toward the island, but the other boats were kayaks being paddled around the idyllic scene. They were watching the fascinating scene below when Mr. Randall broke the silence, reminding them that they needed to press on.

CHAPTER 17
Almost There

Lost Valley Farm

"Mr. Randall, are we almost there yet?" called a tired voice from the rear of the line. This was the second day in the saddle, and a few of the younger, inexperienced students were getting tired of the ride as the day turned warmer and the views were less interesting.

"We're almost there," Mr. Randall replied. "We're looking for the farm as we turn at the next cluster of trees." Now he had the group's interest, and they kept a lookout for the farm buildings and large arena. The horses walked in twos toward the grove of trees that blocked the view.

As the first group of horses rounded the bend, happy voices rang out, "We see the farm." The view opened onto large flat pastures with horses grazing. The grazing horses lifted their heads as they discovered visitors approaching. Immediately the herd started calling to all the riders, and the horses returned the greeting. They passed the pasture, and instantly the large barn was in sight. The horses' chorus alerted everyone that the visiting travelers had arrived. Folks from the main barn came to help the riders find where each horse was to be stabled. There was much excitement as everyone met over the din of horse greetings. There were quick introductions as the hosts tried to get the visitors and their horses to their assigned stalls. Little by little things quieted down, and the riders were free to see where they would camp for their visit.

The Rolling Hills riders gathered in a large meeting room near the large indoor arena. "This feels great," said Alex as he propped himself on a bale of hay. "It feels good to sit on something that isn't moving." The group all laughed. The two-day ride had been great fun, but they were all glad to sit quietly on the bales of motionless hay.

A pleasant lady, the manager of the barn, stood up and welcomed the group. She explained the schedule and how everyone was looking forward to a fun time. A Spanish equestrian group that was visiting Lost Valley would provide an interesting performance. Besides the riding events, there would be a group of dancers. She continued, "You may remember the group that visited Rolling Hills last year and brought their beautiful carriage for a demonstration." She looked around at the nodding heads. "The team is again here again, practicing for their next exhibition … so that the horse team becomes accustomed to performing at different locations. With the team is also a troupe of flamenco dancers. They will perform several items from their program, but they are also going to teach you the popular dance done in Spain called *Sevillanas*. These are the fun to learn fun-to-learn dances that Spaniards love to enjoy at their *fiestas*. Professional dancers perform the intricate steps of Flamenco, but everyone can learn the easy steps of Sevillanas."

Alex whispered to Mr. Randall, "What is a *flamingo* dance*r?* Does it have something to do with pink birds?"

Mr. Randall smiled. "Actually it doesn't have anything to do with pink birds. The word sounds like the name of the pink bird, but it's really a Spanish word that describes a traditional dance called Flamenco. The dancing is performed with guitar music. You'll have plenty of time to meet the group. You remember … this was the group that performed with the carriage and did all those difficult maneuvers. This time they will be staying a little longer than the last time they visited Rolling Hills. They have a new program prepared, so we'll get to see it first."

"Wow, I remember them," Mike interjected. "That was fantastic the way they turned that big carriage around in one small spot. Will they do the same routine again?"

"Yes, they're going to perform some of their routines with some new music," explained Mr. Randall. He had spent time learning about Spain and had lived there for a while. The team members were friends of his, and they had all shared many fun adventures when they had met in Spain. They were now visiting the United States, touring several states and performing a fantastic show.

Alex couldn't contain himself. "Do they have that wonderful carriage with the beautiful horses with them?" Mr. Randall quickly answered their questions about the show because he knew how excited they were about seeing those horses again.

The barn manager continued with a discussion of the coming events. "I know you all must be tired after your long two-day ride, so our students are going to get you all settled, and then we'll meet back in the dining hall for a quick supper and get you tired folks to sleep." She pointed to where all the camping gear was arranged. Everyone got to sleep early that night so they could get up for the next day, which was filled with plans.

CHAPTER 18

The Trail Class Competition

Spanish Horse and Dance Display

"Here they come," called Mike and Alex. They could hardly wait to see the wonderful team of horses that had visited Rolling Hills the year before, when they had spent several days preparing for a performance at a large horse-and-carriage show. The five-horse team practiced at various places to accustom the group to performing at in different locations. One of the difficult aspects of competing with horses is not only getting them to learn routines but to accustom them to performing with strange horses and unexpected conditions. It was a lucky opportunity for the students that the Spanish group was visiting. They also had a Spanish dance group with them that was an addition to the previous performance. The horses and flamenco dancers would perform to live Sevillanas music, characterized by animated, syncopated clapping to guitar sounds. The performance began as the beautifully dressed dancers, costumed in brightly colored, long ruffled dresses, moved with the syncopated guitar beats that signaled the horses' entrance into the arena.

An enthusiastic greeting from the riders watching filled the air as the team of horses and carriage rounded the corner of the arena. The people from Rolling Hills were happy to see their friends. "Gosh, look at their beautiful costumes!" said Cassie. "I had forgotten how exciting their performance was … and with the dancers and music together … it's way cool."

It was a unique sight with the lively music, whirling, vibrant dancers, and magnificently outfitted horses. It was so captivating that the audience began to clap along with the repetitive beat. Sevillanas music is popular at spring fairs in Spanish towns, and each year variations are added. It's similar to square dancing performed to a steady three-beat count. The dancers learn the various patterns with their partner as they perform the steps that always end with an artistic pose.

The group watched, mesmerized by the atmosphere. "It's not often that you get to see a large team of horses perform. It's difficult to transport all that equipment," observed Karl thoughtfully. "Just think about all the difficulty when we take one horse to an event." The older students as part of their equestrian schooling were assigned a horse for the school semester. During that time they studied a discipline such as jumping, cross-country, dressage, driving, vaulting, trail classes, or in- hand halter classes. The older students understood the difficulties of performing in competitions, but also the worries of competing in an unfamiliar place.

The students discussed the uncertainties of horse competitions that are different from classes in riding. The older students who often competed with their horses, presented the younger members with their insights, "You and Cassie will soon be working with Got Carrots to start her in-hand halter classes," said CC as she looked at Annie and Cassie. Both the girls looked surprised. "Of course this will be a great opportunity since you did so much to begin her training. You've been practicing all the parts … so it's time to put them together. Horses do well if they're allowed to learn easy skills one at a time. They don't get so frightened when asked to perform more difficult tasks." The conversation ended. There was a hush as the beautiful team came to a crisp, smart halt in the middle of the arena.

"I think they may perform some of the same routine as last time," whispered Mike.

They all watched as the matched five-horse team moved into a trot around the side of the arena. The horses were all white. They moved in unison, guided by the driver, who held the reins while the background filled with the Sevillanas music that seemed perfectly matched to their cadence.

"How does he do that?" asked Alex. "I have enough difficulty with two reins!"

"Takes a lot of practice. Do you remember why all the horses are white?" Karl questioned.

"I know," said Annie. "It's because they're Andalusians. They're born a strange-looking gray, and as they age, they turn pure white." She stopped and thought. "Yes, these horses must be at least seven or eight years of age to be pure white."

"Right you are."

The team, which was trotting around the arena, again came to a halt in the middle. The audience waited expectantly to see what they would perform next. "I think they're going to do that turn," whispered Mike. The team started around the arena with their shiny harnesses glinting in the sunlight and the tassels on their bridles swinging happily, and performed a series of turns, again coming to the middle of the arena. Slowly the carriage began to pivot and turn without moving forward. The lead horses began to move sideways, swinging the carriage around until they finally faced the opposite direction. As the team once again halted, the spectators energetically clapped their approval.

"It's amazing how they turn the carriage so easily." Mike thought about the classes with the small carriages and how hard he had to concentrate.

"Lots of practice … lots of practice," commented Karl.

Trail Class Event

The team prepared to exit, and it was announced that the next event would start in twenty minutes. The trail class was going to be held in a field near some of the practice arenas that were level or prepared for jumping. This area duplicated some of the terrain that would be found during a trail ride. There was a gradual slope to the pasture and a small stream on the side. On the far side was a wooden gate. Toward the middle there were the familiar poles lying on the ground and bright orange cones arranged.

Shortly the competitors were lined up at the side and the first rider was called to enter the ring. The rider was riding a pleasant-looking smallish brown horse. The helmeted rider approached the rails on the ground, and the horse stepped calmly over each pole. Next was a zigzag through the orange cones at the trot. The rider had to begin the trot at the first cone and end at the last. The rider was having a good ride. She approached the gate and the horse easily stepped sideways to be able to unlatch the gate. After walking through the gate, the horse turned around and sidestepped so the rider could close and latch the gate. There was a low murmur of approval as the rider then approached the area of water. The horse stepped right up to the edge of the water and stopped. It didn't seem that he was going to walk through.

"Oh dear," murmured Cassie, and she held her breath. She thought about the uncertain situations she had been in while learning to ride. Seconds ticked by as the horse checked out the silvery water of the little stream. The rider allowed the horse to lower his head to have a better view.

Karl noted, "Letting the horse see what's ahead is a good approach his ears are forward. Horses change the position of their head so they can see close or far."

"That's really interesting," said Alex. "You learn so many interesting things in those classes you take."

"Don't worry … you'll soon get your chance," replied Karl.

After what seemed a long time, the horse moved easily forward to the rider's command. The trail class finished, and it was time for the next event, which was a group sunset ride.

Sunset Ride

All the riders were going to take a short ride together to see the other side of Lost Valley. The riders from Lost Valley who were hosting the get-together wanted to show the others around the farm. This had become a large group with the riders from the visiting farms. There was lots of noise from the horses as they called to each other. "Even horses enjoy meeting new friends," noted Annie as their group followed Mr. Randall. The ride would only go to the lake for the beautiful sunset and view of the mountains. The trip back up to the main farm would follow along the road lined with the Lost Valley pasture of breeding mares with their foals that was at the lower edge of the farm. Lost Valley was similar to Rolling Hills in that it was close to the large open range of the valley.

"Maybe we'll see the wild horses from the open range," commented Mike, who hadn't forgotten about their Mystery Mare and where she might have come from. He wanted to get a closer look at the wild horses to see if any were similar in appearance to the Mystery Mare.

"And don't forget about Got Carrots, our little filly saved near Rolling Hills Farm … we don't know anything about her."

The story of the beautiful Mystery Mare now safely stalled at Rolling Hills was certainly a mystery. She had been found hurt with the wild horses on the open range between the two farms. It was strange that she seemed to know Got Carrots the filly rescued by Annie and Cassie. There were many questions about the two horses' connection to the wild herd.

Mr. Randall led the riders quietly down the lane to an ideal place to watch the beautiful sunset. They had to hurry to reach the viewing area, because sunsets take only a little more than two minutes. The group stood quietly at the edge of the Lost Valley farm's lake, watching the gold rays at sunset. Almost as if on command everything was quiet, as if there were no horses or riders. They were all taking in the beginning of the beautiful sunset, when suddenly the sound of approaching horses could be faintly heard coming from the far side of the lake. Now in the drawing deep shadows, the outline of a herd of horses could barely be seen as they almost soundlessly approached the lake.

There were quiet whispers among the group because no one wanted to surprise or frighten the wild horses. Mike whispered, "It's them … Look, it's the wild horses." They all watched in surprised amazement as the herd quietly lined the lake and began to drink. The drinking went on for some time, and then, just as suddenly as the horses had appeared in an unhurried movement, they vanished in slow motion into the fading light.

Chapter 19
Back at Rolling Hills

Rider Practice

Before the riders could absorb all the wonderful events of the previous days, the trail ride was over. Horses were loaded into the large transport for the return trip to Rolling Hills, and riders were driven back to the farm. Tired but still excited about the trail ride, the students were happy to sleep in their cabins.

As if a wonderful dream, the time flew by. There were several more days of classes, and a schooling show for halter and trail ride events was planned. People from the other farms they had visited were going to join the Rolling Hills farm for a picnic and event day. Got Carrots was going to perform in her first halter class. Annie and Cassie were busy working with her each day. They practiced standing and walking on cue. Besides the halter class they were going to do a trail ride event. Each student had been assigned a horse and was busily practicing. Everyone was meeting in the large arena for final lessons and practice.

The older students who were practicing their teaching skills were responsible for coaching the younger students. Again the team of four was working with Karl, one of their favorite student instructors. They had happily become accustomed to working with him over the past two riding courses. He had an easygoing, quiet way of teaching that made everyone feel comfortable and not afraid of making mistakes. The older students were taught techniques for working with the younger students so that they learned new skills and felt comfortable working with their horses.

Alex, Mike, Cassie, and Annie were lined up with their horses, and Karl was giving instructions. They listened attentively as he reviewed their previous classes.

"This is going to be our basic trail course that you have all practiced." He looked at the group and saw happy faces except for Cassie. Noting her apprehension, he proceeded with the lesson. "All the horses are competent with this lesson, but being horses, they sometimes are unsure of themselves just like we are. Part of the partnership of horse and rider is to build this communication, so the rider must be clear about the directions given to the horse. Especially with trail riding, the horses are constantly being exposed to new things that may surprise them. Part of why we practice in the arena is to have a safe place to expose the horses to things that may be new." Karl waited to see if there were any questions.

"Our mounts have been practicing trail lessons as school horses here at Rolling Hills, but that doesn't mean they might suddenly not recognize something in the arena. One of the differences between the group trail ride and doing a trail ride event is that you and the horse are alone in the arena." Karl paused while the students considered this thought.

The group went through the trail practice effortlessly, and Karl reminded them how much they had all learned. Each student individually went successfully through the course of obstacles. The practice session ended. All the riders prepared their horses for grooming and the evening feed. It was almost time for the evening meal and the normal fun get-together. There was always lots of exciting talk, and that night, much of the discussion was about the trail ride to Lost Valley and the upcoming event.

Group Meeting

As Mr. Randall joined his lesson group, the enthusiastic questions began all at once. "Wait a moment…one at a time," he said.

After Mr. Randall answered most of the questions, the group sat around their normal meeting table. They were chatting about all the exciting events when Mike brought out the old newspaper he had carefully saved from the cabin and spread it out on the table. "What do you think about this?" he asked.

"That's very interesting and a piece of history about the area we just traveled by horseback," Mr. Randall replied. "Our short experience wasn't very different from that of the working folks on horseback who traveled from farm to farm. They used the same trail we followed. The difference is that we had it a little easier by not having to pack all of our food and necessities along by mules or wagons." The group gathered around the table and scrutinized the old frayed piece of newspaper. One by one they observed different items on the opened page.

"Of course the first important clue about this newspaper was that it was used to help make the cabin more comfortable by sealing out the cold night winds that often sweep through this valley." Mr. Randall said, "The spaces between the logs in the cabin were stuffed with mud and any other items that were available to keep out the winter chill."

"Look how cheap all the food was," Alex noticed, looking at the paper's advertisements. "Even candy was cheap."

"The stories are interesting too. Seems as if this paper was published in a fairly large town," said Mike.

The lively conversation about the old newspaper continued until it was almost time to turn in. The group turned their attention to Miss Katy when she walked up to their table. Everyone suddenly became silent as they waited to hear the latest news about Jasmine.

"Jasmine will be able to come back to the farm tomorrow," Miss Katy said.

The group erupted into an elated cheer.

She continued, "That is the good news, Jasmine is on the mend but"—she looked at the suddenly apprehensive faces—"she is going to have to stay extremely quiet in my office. There can be no more excursions around the barn, at least for quite a long time. This may be difficult for our active little cat. We'll all have to make sure she stays in the closed office. We have to see how this goes before we know how much activity she'll be able to handle."

Everyone seemed unusually quiet. Alex was the first to break the silence. "At least we won't have to worry about where she is," he said on a positive note, to which everyone silently agreed.

Jasmine's wanderings had caused much worry to the folks at the farm. The last time she had climbed up to the highest part of the old barn, she had caused everyone to be anxious while they hunted all over the farm. Everyone had been worried about her safety for several days. It seemed that Jasmine was rapidly using up her "nine lives." There is an English proverb that says that cats have nine lives: three lives to play, three lives to stray, and three lives to hang around and get attention.

Annie said, "I've read that if cats fall, they have the ability to twist themselves and land on their feet."

Miss Katy nodded, "yes that is certainly true because of their flexible backbones. They have the ability to right themselves, but animal clinics often treat cats for falls … as what happened to Jasmine." She continued, "It's very important that she stays quiet for awhile to allow her hip to heal. Most likely during the fall, Jasmine's hip joint was pushed out of the bone holding it together."

The solemn faces reflected the gravity of what Miss Katy had explained.

She hurriedly said, "It's not as grave as you may think. In the operation the veterinarian clipped off the joint, leaving the bone in the large hip muscle. The muscle takes over in place of the previous bone connection. So ..." She paused to see if everyone understood. "Jasmine's hurt leg is now free in her large hip muscle, and little by little the muscles will tighten around the bone supporting it." Again she paused, and then she emphasized, "And this is where all of you need to help Jasmine recover the use of her leg."

This time it was Mike who voiced what the group was thinking. "What can we do to help?" Mike was always thinking of ways to make things better; he was a problem-solver at heart.

Miss Katy explained the physical therapy that Jasmine would need. "We'll set up a schedule like we do for all the important stable activities, and gently exercise Jasmine's leg. She is doing very well. The clinic kept her several days to stabilize her since they knew she was coming back to the farm and would have to be contained from running around for several weeks." She noticed that all the students were looking relieved that Jasmine would make a recovery. "I'm sure Jasmine would love to see you for a few minutes ... if it's okay with Mr. Randall."

"We were talking about some of the interesting discoveries the group made on the trail ride," Mr. Randall said. "But I'm sure there is plenty of time to continue this discussion tomorrow." He could see that the students wanted to see Jasmine. "Good enough ... we'll continue this tomorrow at breakfast and prepare the schedule for the trail riding events." With this final comment, Cassie, Annie, Alex, and Mike gathered their belongings and followed Miss Katy over to her office.

When the foursome arrived, they could see Jasmine sleeping on a small bed of blankets. Even though everyone was quiet, Jasmine lifted her head and made a small sound. "She is taking medication to help her," Miss Katy said. "We're hoping she stays quiet so the healing process is successful." Jasmine promptly put her head back down on the blanket but kept a watchful eye open.

"She looks much better," said Annie, "considering how close we came to not finding her."

"I'll give Mr. Randall a schedule that fits in with your riding schedule. Each of you can work with me so we can practice together." Miss Katy noticed that Cassie looked worried. "Don't worry—this is easy … Jasmine knows all of you, which makes it perfect. Basically all we have to do is gently move her leg so she doesn't lose flexibility. The clinic tells me that cats do so well, they can run and do everything they did before. The muscle takes over for the bone connection."

"Gosh, I hope Jasmine doesn't keep doing what she did before," said Cassie. Then she thought maybe she had said something wrong.

"I know what you mean, Cassie," Miss Katy said. "It's a real concern with all of our animals … to allow them freedom but keep them safe. Don't worry … we'll come up with a plan," she reassured the group. As a second thought Miss Katy added, "Sometimes animals are pretty smart and solve the problem for us. You all run along and get ready for tomorrow … we'll talk more in the morning."

"Good night, Miss Katy, and thank you for taking good care of Jasmine," said Annie, echoing the thanks from the group.

CHAPTER 20
Trail Class Event

Final Competition

The riders were looking forward to the coming events as they gathered for breakfast. Talk about the competition was animated. Besides the trail class, there was to be a halter class. A halter class demonstrates horses that are led and not ridden. There are skills that must be learned by both the horse and the person leading the horse, or the handler.

In some events the horses are judged on breeding and conformation. However, there are halter classes that judge young people on their ability to groom and present their horse. These horses are often not old enough to be ridden, but they gain skills on the ground and learn to understand the handler's commands. Besides immaculate grooming, showmanship is also important. The horses must learn to stand quietly and walk or trot in a pattern along with the handler.

"Everyone looks ready to go." The group tidied up the breakfast dishes and quickly sat down to listen to Mr. Randall as he began to describe the schedule. "We're going to have a visit from the club riders from the Lost Valley farm we visited."

There were pleased looks and Alex asked, "When are they coming?"

"We have a fun schooling show planned for Sunday. The Lost Valley riders will have their horses trucked over on Saturday afternoon. They'll spend Saturday night camping here with a campfire party." This information received a happy cheer from the group.

"That is way cool," said Cassie. "What kind of competitions will we do … the same trail classes that they did at Lost Valley?"

"Yes, you students have had lots of practice, so this will be a perfect time to try your skills in a competition. We're also going to do a halter class for a few of our young horses such as Got Carrots. I know you have been practicing with her. This will be a good opportunity for the horses to perform in a different situation, with the visitor horses included. You remember how interested our horses were to arrive at the Lost Valley Farm and meet new horses."

The riders remembered the noisy nickering from the barn horses and the grazing horses outside. Cassie and Annie exchanged glances and thought about all the work they did practicing with Got Carrots and their school horse mounts. Cassie had been working with Little Pony and had gained vast confidence in her riding ability. Little Pony was one of the Rolling Hills school horses and an excellent teacher with his patient manners. The school horses at the farm were all trained, so the students had the opportunity to learn from not only the teachers but the horses as well.

The day finally arrived and everyone was ready for the fun day of events. There would be the trail ride competition with a set of obstacles set up in the arena. There would be several classes with easy obstacles and a more advanced course with difficult obstructions such as a wooden bridge. Many of the older students had spent much time practicing with their assigned horses. It would be fun to see the advanced classes. There would also be a halter class where the horses would be walked in hand to demonstrate obedience to commands. This would be the first time for Annie and Cassie to show Got Carrots. They were both anticipating the events, spending a great amount of energy working with their filly.

Jasmine was also on the mend, and the students faithfully performed her leg exercises, hoping that she would eventually regain the use of her leg. Each student took a scheduled session, gently moving Jasmine's leg so she could continue to use it. Many cats regain total use of their leg as the muscle takes over for support.

On Saturday the horse van arrived with the horses and riders from Lost Valley. The horses were unloaded and shown their stables. Students were assigned guests to show around the farm.

Soon everyone gathered in the dining hall for a snack before the afternoon events and evening barbecue. Mrs. R made the necessary announcement about the events and schedules amid much excitement. The group tidied up the room and met in the main barn while the older students prepared their mounts. The afternoon event was going to have an advanced schooling show to give the riders an opportunity to prepare their horses for future competition. Schooling shows are designed to help horses and riders to practice showing.

The younger students from both farms would have an opportunity to see the older students perform at a challenging level. Practicing with trail obstacles in an arena helps riders practice skills needed on the open trail. This advanced class was going to have a mock gate and a wooden bridge, and would require walking and trotting over poles of different heights.

Sunday's Event

Sunday began with a fun breakfast in the dining hall. Many friends and family members of the riders were arriving to watch the day's events. It was exciting for the riders to have an audience. The first class was going to be the beginners' trail class. Cassie, Mike, and Alex had prepared their horses and stood with them, waiting for their turn. It had been decided that since the grooming for Got Carrots would take time, Cassie would do the trail class and Annie the halter class.

Mrs. R announced each rider in turn as they went around the course. Several of the Lost Valley riders went around the course, but each horse made a small mistake, losing points for the rider. It's always more difficult being the visiting competitor, but all the riders realized that practice is well worth the effort. Mr. Randall was standing next to the group as Cassie was called to start the course. "Now relax and have fun with Little Pony—he knows how to do the course," he encouraged her. He could see she was nervous, because she was quietly whistling her little song. This was good practice for Cassie, because she often lacked confidence in herself.

"Okay, Little Pony," Cassie whispered. "I know we can do this together." She gave him the command to walk on and began toward their first obstacle. *Encourage Little Pony to walk straight over the poles,* Cassie told herself. She approached the poles but felt a bit unsure. She thought to herself, *If I'm unsure, Little Pony will be uncertain. I have to clearly tell him the command to walk on.* She gave Little Pony the command and he stepped toward the poles, looked at them, waited a second, and then walked right over.

The rest of the team watching all looked knowingly at one another … they recognized how Cassie felt. Riders have to work each horse partnership with positive practice. They all knew that clear communication was important. Everyone knew how hard the team had practiced with the horses. They eagerly awaited the halter class and the entrance of Annie and Got Carrots.

Annie stood with Got Carrots eagerly waiting for their turn in the arena. It seemed like only yesterday that she stood looking at what they thought was a pile of rags. She thought of how attached to Got Carrots she had become as she helped nurse her back to health. Each time she'd taken classes at Rolling Hills, she had spent a lot of time working with Got Carrots. Now they were standing side by side, waiting for their cue to enter the arena for their first schooling show. The older students were to present their horses in halter training, and then it would be their turn.

She turned and looked at Got Carrots standing very patiently, waiting for Annie to give a command. Annie had small pieces of carrots in her pocket to reward her for obedient behavior.

Mrs. R was heard announcing, "We now have one of our youngest horses, Got Carrots." There was polite applause. "We're not sure how old she is, since she was found separated from the herd of wild horses. Since you saw her almost one year ago, Got Carrots has been practicing basic commands with our young rider Annie. Please welcome Got Carrots."

Suddenly there was the noise of applause from the audience and Got Carrots momentarily looked apprehensive. On cue Annie calmly said, "Walk on." Got Carrots immediately focused her attention on Annie and began to walk next to her. They approached the judge, who asked Annie to have Got Carrots stand so she could walk around the filly to evaluate her conformation.

"Stand," said Annie. Got Carrots immediately took a position at attention, holding her head perfectly while watching Annie.

"Please walk your horse around the triangle, and return and stand here again," said the judge.

Annie gave the command to walk on, and Got Carrots obediently began to walk along with her. They arrived back near the judge, and Annie gave the filly the command to stand. Got Carrots again stood with her attention focused on Annie.

For Annie the short course with Got Carrots flew by as they performed all the exercises. They completed the requirements and were suddenly walking back to the stalls. Annie caught sight of her smiling parents and Cassie's aunt waving proudly.

Back at the stall, she said, "Wow, Got Carrots, we did it." She looked at her expressive face and handed a carrot to the patiently waiting filly.

CHAPTER 21

Tour of the Stables and Goodbyes

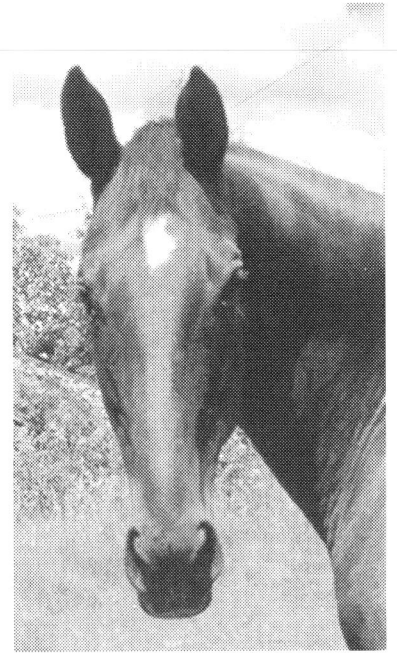

See You Later

The Lost Valley riders were busily getting their horses ready for the van to take the horses back to the valley. After they were all safely loaded, the group walked back to the main barn to meet their new friends from Rolling Hills and take a tour of the stables. A tall girl named Karen came energetically walking up the path to meet Annie and Cassie. "Well, it seems my horse didn't want to go home," she said, laughing. "He's so particular about checking everything out to make sure it's okay … and then he walked right in. You remember the trail class at Lost Valley."

"Yes," Cassie said. "I remember because I thought when your horse paused …"

Karen filled in the rest for Cassie, "… he wouldn't walk across the little bit of water. I was worried, so I am always trying to be patient and give him a chance to check it out … then he's just fine. He's a wonderfully trained school horse, and I'm learning lots from him."

"I held my breath while you were standing near the water, but Karl, one of our teachers, noticed your horse was attentive, and as soon as he lowered his head, he walked right across."

Several of the other visitors joined with the Rolling Hills students as they walked through the main stable, meeting the horses. There was happy conversation as the past horse adventures were discussed. Karen and Cassie had a fun exchange about their school mounts Little Pony and Firefly. Cassie and Karen were joined by Annie, who suggested that they visit the back barn near Miss Katy's office and see how Jasmine was doing. The trio walked down the long row of horses until they came to the section where horses needing special attention were kept. Miss Katy's door was closed to make sure Jasmine wouldn't go on another excursion. They looked through the window into the office to discover that Jasmine was sound asleep.

"She's pretty tired and taking medicine to heal after the hip operation." They told Karen the tale of Jasmine. Karen responded that they had several barn cats at Lost Valley that all the students cared for.

"Got Carrots and the hurt mare found with the wild horses are kept back here in the separate stalls," Annie commented as she led the way.

As soon as the horses heard footsteps, they called, one with a normal nicker and another in a high-pitched sound.

The trio stood in front of the two stalls, reviewing the story of how the filly had been found after a storm and the mare several months later when Annie and Cassie flew on a trip to visit the area between the farms where the wild horses roamed. They were standing there chatting when Karen suddenly said, "This mare looks very much like some of our brood mares." She looked intently at Got Carrots and the Mystery Mare. "She has a fine, delicate muzzle and expressive eyes that leave little doubt that she's a mare." They were thinking about her words when the call for the Lost Valley riders to leave was heard.

"This was so … way cool. We'll have to keep in touch," said Cassie.

Annie added, "We should get the two schools to do this again. Pretty soon we have the summer vacation to look forward to."

They waved to Karen as she hurried off to join her group. The girls stood in front of the horses' stalls, silently looking at their cherished friends. The horses came to the stall door as if to say goodbye. Quietly the girls looked at each other and understood that this wasn't really goodbye but *hasta luego*. As Mr. Randall always said, friends don't have to say goodbye forever—only until the next time.

"We better catch up with our ride too," Annie said. The girls had all their belongings ready to go. "It all went by too quickly," she lamented.

Annie's dad helped them put their things into the trunk. "You two really did great in the trail ride and halter class."

"I am so impressed to see how confident you both are with the horses," commented Aunt Emma. "Cassie, you and Little Pony are quite the team … Annie, you and Got Carrots have learned all the basics. It was terrific to see how much you've studied during the three riding sessions."

The girls sank into the comfortable backseat as the car slowly wound its way down the farm road. There were happy thoughts as Annie and Cassie thought about their wonderful adventure and what would come next at Rolling Hills with Got Carrots and the Mystery Mare.

ABOUT THE AUTHOR

Patti Dammier has been an educator of horses and riders for more than thirty years. Her experience in Europe and the United States provides a broad equestrian perspective. During twenty-three years overseas, while an elementary school teacher, she studied equestrian disciplines in Spain, Portugal, England, and Germany. Many of the story situations in this book are based on her real-life experiences.

With a PhD in psychology, Patti is an expert in educational curriculum, psychology, and applied behavior analysis. Based on her background, she uses her expertise to write about horse training based on scientific theories and educational methods. Besides working with her own European horses, she continues to help retrain rescued horses. She would like to promote the training of horses through sound educational principles.

The focus of her first book is about "a positive method for training horses." She believes that horse-training literature should encourage the equestrian toward that goal. Patti would like to promote the use of valuable educational and scientific information to be applied to both fiction and nonfiction writing for the education of both horse and rider.

AFTERWORDS

There are many exciting equestrian sports that aren't promoted by the mass media. Ideally the thoughts briefly described in this fun story about animals and horses will provide an incentive to find more information.

The sport of driving is an approach that beginning horse lovers may learn to acquire equestrian skills in a safe manner. As described in the story, people who have not had any previous horse experience may safely begin their education by learning to drive carriages. Driving also provides access for many would-be equestrians who aren't able to mount a horse.

The disciplines of dressage and jumping are often viewed as sports that aren't available to the average horse lover. The pretrained competitive horse model has gained acceptance, and many readers might assume that the enjoyment of these activities isn't possible. There are many examples of rejected, rescued horses, or average horses that have turned out to be exceptional mounts through systematic training. Fine horses are often overlooked because their owners lacked the time, knowledge, and patience needed for training. This story provides interesting ideas for horse lovers.

Additional Resources

1. *Got Carrots? Rescued Horse: The Beginning of the Adventure*

2. Got *Carrots? Rescued Horse: The Winter Vacation*
   www.GotCarrotsRescuedHorse.com

3. *Got Carrots? Behavior Modification for Horses: A Positive Method for Training Horses*
   www.GotCarrots.com
   www.BehaviorModificationHorses.com

4. *Got Carrots? Horse Makeovers: A Positive Method for Training Horses*
   www.GotCarrots.com